FUN GUIDE TO NEW YORK CITY 2024

MICHAEL D. KOCH & JURI KOCH

ILLUSTRATIONS BY MICHAEL D. KOCH

(QR CODE)
VISIT OUR LINKS ON LINKTREE:
linktr.ee / funfunnewyork

The Fun Fun Robot

funfunnewyork.com

ISBN: 9798880010523
Published by Fun Fun New York

TABLE OF CONTENTS

TABLE OF CONTENTS

ABOUT THE GUIDE

GUIDE FOCUSES ON MANHATTAN - WHAT TO DO AND
WHERE TO GO IN EACH PART OF THE CITY

GIVES YOU AFFORDABLE OPTIONS AND GREAT CHOICES
SO YOU CAN DO LESS SEARCHING AND HAVE MORE FUN!

FIND SMALL BUSINESSES IN NEW YORK CITY THAT YOU
CAN SUPPORT TO KEEP THINGS OPEN & AUTHENTIC

TIPS ON USING THE FUN GUIDE

ALL LISTINGS UPDATED, ADDED TO & CURRENT FOR 2024
All listings have been checked and rechecked to keep track as best we could for
updates, closings as well as new listings for each neighborhood as of February
2024. The good news is a lot of the regulars and newcomers are still here and
going strong but a few longtime favorites in the city did close up shop last year,
even though they might continue on in some form or other.

So here's a toast to places like the Papaya King, Ceci-Cela Patisserie, Neil's Coffee Shop,
JHU Comic Books and B&N Tribeca. Thank you for all you've done to make the
city a much more enjoyable place.

DIRECTIONS / SUBWAY
Each neighborhood listed comes with quick and easy subway directions. Make sure to
pay attention to whether the train is "**uptown**" or "**downtown**" for the proper direction.

In general,
Uptown is past 34ʰ St - past Midtown & 57ᵗʰᵗ St to Upper East Side, Upper West
Side, Central Park, Harlem & the Bronx.

Downtown is below 34ᵗʰ St - going towards Flatiron, Chelsea, East & West Village,
NYU, Lower East Side, Chinatown, Tribeca & Wall St heading towards Brooklyn.

MIDTOWN
Midtown in New York is so big that we broke it down into its 6 respective parts
Each area of Midtown is treated like its own neighborhood with its own offerings :

(1) *Midtown - 57th St - Central Park*   (4) *Midtown - Times Sq -Theater District*
(2) *Midtown - 5th Ave - Midtown East*   (5) *Midtown - Midtown West -Hudson Yds*
(3) *Midtown - Grand Central St - 42nd St* (6) *Midtown - 34th St- Garment District*

ABOUT THE GUIDE

COFFEE
The main goal for this section is to track down the best coffeeshops or the most solid options in each NYC neighborhood that doesn't go by the name "Starbucks". Not that Starbucks isn't a decent choice (as we do list some here) but there are so many Starbucks franchises in the city that they would overtake any coffeeshop listing simply by documenting them. So we looked for other coffee places that have more of the character and flavor of each neighborhood while supporting the vibrant coffee culture in New York.

Note about coffeeshops
We note at the end of our coffeeshop & cafe listings if doesn't have Wifi or bathrooms which is valuable info for those of us in the city who want to work, hang out or write that screenplay with a drink in hand. There are plenty of Starbucks with all these amenities but they get crowded fast. Most coffee places have the overhead of high rents or small spaces to stay in these neighborhoods so they can't always offer these options, need faster turnover or just set up for grab & go. So we try to credit those who offer these appreciated extras or give the heads up if they don't before you get there.

TEA PLACES
We've been keeping track of the flourishing tea culture in New York since our first published Fun Guide. Even in that short amount of time, that scene has exploded with more coffeeshops & cafes listing as many tea options as coffee choices nowadays.

EATS, RESTAURANTS & BARS
Price range for eats, restaurants and bars in general for each area. Even though everything overall is more expensive these days, these categories still apply for the most part:

($) cheaper places
($$) affordable options
($$$-$$$$) to note the worthwhile, pricier places

ABOUT THE GUIDE
When I worked as a designer in different parts of the city, I was always looking for advice about what's fun to to do in the area, the good places to eat or have a coffee. It turned into a pretty involved research project where I was doing a lot of guidebook-buying, magazine-reading, website-visiting and constant asking around about all these interesting neighborhoods I was working in.

My wife Juri and I thought that there has got to be an easier way to do this instead of constantly cycling through phone apps —a kind of decoder ring for NYC that's current, relevant, researched and most of all, simplified!

First we did a website that eventually became the dream book you're reading now, the one I wished I had back then. A simplified guide that was meant to serve New Yorkers as much as those visiting the city. We hope you find this to be a reliable companion that gets you off to a running start to enjoy all this city has to offer in a more informed, affordable and authentic way. - MDK

UPPER WEST SIDE

quick directions
Take 1, 2, 3 train uptown to 72nd St Broadway stop [w72nd/Broadway]

COFFEE

Irving Farm Coffee Roasters (coffee shop, w79th/Broadway)
[224 W 79th St] *coffee, pastry & eats in a roomy, brownstone basement place w/ seating in front and back (no Wifi)*

Daily Provisions - Upper West Side (gourmet cafe, Amsterdam/w78th)
[375 Amsterdam Ave] *good-sized cafe & bakery by restauranteur who started Shake Shack, gourmet coffee, pastries, cookies, breakfast & comfort foods w/sidewalk seating, Wifi*

Plowshares Coffee Roasters (coffee shop, Broadway/w104th)
[2730 Broadway] *solid mid-sized coffee shop near Bloomingdale's Outlet store that serves its own coffee brand & pastries in a well-maintained space w/seating, Wifi (no bathroom)*

Birch Coffee (coffee shop, Columbus/w96th)
[750 Columbus Ave] *generous-sized coffee shop that serves food & pastries, good to hang out or work at, roomy w/seating (no Wifi)*

Joe Coffee Company (coffee shop, Columbus/w85th)
[514 Columbus Ave] *mid-sized coffee shop, pastries, reliable place with limited seating (no Wifi)*

Starbucks (coffee shop, West End Ave/e61st)
[21 West End Ave] *spacious Starbucks in less trafficked area w/lounge seating, relaxed & roomy, near Fordham Univ. Lincoln Center campus, Wifi*

TEA

Alice's Tea Cup Chapter 1 (tea room, famous scones, w73rd/Columbus)
[102 W 73rd St] *tea room and breakfast place, famous for its scones and Alice in Wonderland theme w/tea drinks, breakfast, sandwiches, pastries and whimsical decor, cozy spot for a tea get-together*

Floating Mountain Tea House (tea house & art gallery, w72nd/Broadway)
[239 W 72nd St #2FL] *elegant, serene and stylish tea room with art gallery, serves Chinese herbal tea in a calming space with artistically presented tea sets*

Chalait UWS (matcha tea & all-day breakfast cafe, Amsterdam/w82nd)
[461 Amsterdam Ave] *cafe specializing in matcha teas, hot teas, coffee, breakfast all-day, sandwiches & grain bowls in a nice, well put-together space*

EATS

($)

Sal & Carmine's Pizza (old school slice, Broadway/w102nd)
[2671 Broadway] *old school NY pizza parlor that's considered best slice in UWS, has seating inside, regularly featured on many best NYC slice lists*

Levain Bakery (famous bakery known for its cookies, w74th/Amsterdam)
[167 W 74th St - original location] *famous bakery known for its cookies, considered best cookies in the city (esp. chocolate chip walnut) Also has baked goods, breads, scones, this is the original bakery at small location so grab & go*
Note: *A bigger, newer location that's better for lines and seating is just a few blocks away at 351 Amsterdam Ave, Amsterdam/w77th*

UPPER WEST SIDE

Levain Bakery - Upper West Side (famous bakery known for its cookies, newer location, Amsterdam/w77th)
[351 Amsterdam Ave - newer, bigger location] *famous bakery known for its cookies, considered best cookies in the city (esp. chocolate chip walnut) Also has baked goods, breads, scones. This is the newer, bigger location offering more seating & space compared to the original, smaller bakery location a few blocks away on w74th St*

Absolute Bagels (famous NYC bagel shop near Columbia University, Broadway/108th)
[2788 Broadway] *house-made & hand rolled rolled bagels, considered among the very best in the city - popular egg bagel or cream cheese bagels, highly regarded, usually has lines, cash only!*

Gray's Papaya (classic NYC hot dog joint, Broadway/w80th)
[2090 Broadway] *NYC hot dog joint famous for its inexpensive hot dog specials & celebrated papaya drinks, centrally located, well-known & popular*

Whole Foods Market (lower level of Whole Foods, ColumbusCircle/w59th)
[10 Columbus Circle] *food court at Whole Foods with hot food, salad bar, prepared foods, seating and booths in lower level area, often crowded*

($$)

Community Food & Juice (American, brkfst/brunch spot, Broadway/w112th)
[2893 Broadway] *popular UWS/Morningside Heights comfort food restaurant with breakfast & brunch, blueberry pancakes, brioche French toast, biscuit sandwich in a close-quartered dining space, owned by Clinton St. Baking Company, well regarded*

Jin Ramen Upper West Side (Japanese ramen & rice bowl joint, Amsterdam/w82nd)
[462 Amsterdam] *Japanese ramen, rice bowls & comfort foods in modest space with casual setting, table & bar seating, often on Michelin Bib Gourmand list for affordable standouts*

Shake Shack - Upper West Side (burger place, Columbus/w77th)
[366 Columbus Ave] *popular NYC burger chain, often on best burger lists, has light-filled window area seating on street level in limited space, can get crowded*

Zabar's (famous grocery & deli shop, Broadway/w80th)
[2245 Broadway] *famous gourmet deli, grocery & home items store in UWS - sells cheeses, olives, pastries, breads, cured fish, smoked salmons, lox , has grab & go eatery place on corner that sells knishes, potato latkes, breakfast & bagel sandwiches*

Thai Market (authentic Thai food in market-style setting, Amsterdam/w107th)
[960 Amsterdam Ave] *bustling & popular market-style Thai restaurant, known for it's authentic Thai food -Pad Thai, noodle & rice dishes, also has good lunch specials*

Orwasher's Artisan Bakery (sandwiches, popular jelly donuts, e78th/2nd)
[440 Amsterdam Ave] *artisan bakery in corner store space, popular for its hand-filled fresh-baked jelly donuts, also makes breads, croissants & muffins w/seating, well regarded*

Luke's Lobster Upper West Side (Maine lobster rolls, Amsterdam/w81st)
[426 Amsterdam] *rustic UWS outpost of Luke's Lobster in a modest-sized interior, popular lobster rolls ,seafood & chowder, w/limited seating*

Sushi Yasaka (affordable Japanese sushi, w72nd/Broadway)
[251 W 72nd St] *affordable & solid Japanese sushi restaurant in UWS, known for its quality sushi & omakase at reasonable prices, well regarded, reservations*

($$$)

Maison Pickle (cocktail bar & American comfort food, Broadway/w84th)
[2315 Broadway] *cocktail bar & restaurant with ambience, jar-covered walls, interior booths w/table seating below an upper-level wrapping staircase, Serves hearty French dip sandwiches w/American comfort foods - mac & cheese, southern skillet dishes and challah French toast*

Sushi of Gari UWS (fancy Japanese sushi, Columbus/w77th)
[370 Columbus Ave] *Japanese sushi restaurant, part of a mini-group of NY Gari sushi restaurants, often in the top NYC sushi lists w/chef omakase, reservations*

DRINKS & BARS

($$)

Bob's Your Uncle (laid-back craft beer bar, Columbus/w105th)
[929 Columbus Ave] *easygoing bar with framed pictures of famous Bob's on the wall, rustic dimly-lit space with a laid back vibe, craft beers and games, happy hour specials daily except Fri nights*

e's Bar (retro rock dive bar, Amsterdam/w84th)
[511 Amsterdam Ave] *solid casual bar offering music, bar food, classic board games & Tuesday trivia nights in a roomy industrial loft space that has booths in back*

UPPER WEST SIDE

The Dead Poet (Irish pub, Amsterdam/w81st)
[450 Amsterdam Ave] *old school Irish pub decorated with poets & books on the wall in a long bar space w/chunky tables where you can comfortably down a pint of Guinness*

($$$)

Maison Pickle (cocktail bar & American comfort food, Broadway/w84th)
[2315 Broadway] *cocktail bar & restaurant with ambience, jar-covered walls, interior booths w/table seating below an upper-level wrapping staircase, Serves hearty French dip sandwiches w/American comfort foods - mac & cheese, southern skillet dishes and challah French toast*

SHOPPING

Shops at Columbus Circle (Time Warner Center, ColumbusCrcl/w59th)
[10 Columbus Circle] *mall complex in Time Warner Center at Columbus Circle featuring shops like Williams Sonoma cookware, H&M clothing, J.Crew clothing, TUMI luggage, Jo Malone London fragrances, Alo yoga activeware, Lululemon activewear, La Maison du Chocolat, Ladurée macarons, Moleskin stationary, luxury brand stores, fancy restaurants, Jazz at Lincoln Center & a Whole Foods on the basement level*

Bloomingdale's Outlet (outlet store of Bloomingdales, Broadway/w72nd)
[2085 Broadway] *outlet store with deals, discounts & bargains from the Bloomingdales department stores, corner store next to the 72nd St train station*

Barnes & Noble bookstore (big bookstore, Broadway/w82nd)
[2289 Broadway] *Barnes & Noble bookstore of Upper West Side, roomy B&N with a Starbucks cafe upstairs and event space*

Book Culture (independent bookstore in Morningside Heights, w112th/Broadway)
[536 W 112 St] *charming independent bookstore chain, NY book lovers destination, carefully curated and well ordered*

Zabar's (famous grocery & deli shop, Broadway/w80th)
[2245 Broadway] *famous gourmet deli, grocery & home items store in UWS - sells cheeses, olives, pastries, breads, cured fish, smoked salmons, lox , has grab & go eatery place on corner that sells knishes, potato latkes, breakfast & bagel sandwiches*

Grand Bazaar NYC (indoor-outdoor Sunday flea market, w77th/Columbus)
[100 W 77th St] *indoor/outdoor large flea market where vendors sell used & vintage goods, art and crafts, with artisanal food stands, every Sunday year round from 10-5*

OUTDOOR PUBLIC SPACES & MANHATTAN VIEWS

Central Park (grand city park of NYC, w59th/Central Pk thru w110th/5th)
[59th St to 110th St, 5th Ave to Central Park W] *one of the most famous parks in the world, Central Park is a grand, magnificent and very designed swath of nature right in the middle of the city. A masterpiece of landscape architecture and urban planning created over 150 years ago by Frederick Law Olmstead & Calvert Vaux. It spans 51 blocks from 59th St to 110th St along Fifth Avenue. Lots to do in the park but most of all, it's a nice walk on a beautiful day, free park Wifi*

Riverside Park Promenade (waterfront park on Hudson, Riverside Dr/w83rd)
[Riverside Drive at 83rd St] *river walk and waterfront park by the Hudson River, good for walks or running, nice scenery especially at sunset*

Lincoln Center for the Performing Arts (Lincoln Plaza, Columbus/w63rd)
[70 Lincoln Center Plaza] *the major cultural center of NYC and great home of the arts with the Metropolitan Opera, NY Philharmonic, Alice Tully Hall, Juilliard School, NYC Ballet, Jazz at Lincoln Center & Film at Lincoln Center, can get tickets online*

FUN STUFF

AMC 84th Street 6 (movie theater, Broadway/84th)
[2310 Broadway] *AMC multiplex theater with large comfy, cushioned recliner seats w/ legroom, assigned seating and a good reputation for a city movie theater, w/IMAX*

Beacon Theatre (concert music hall, Broadway/w74th)
[2124 Broadway] *famous 1920's UWS concert hall and opulent theater with exquisite detailing, balcony seating & superior acoustics. Still a destination spot for headline musicians & entertainers*

Grand Bazaar NYC (indoor-outdoor Sunday flea market, w77th/Columbus)
[100 W 77th St] *indoor/outdoor large flea market where vendors sell used & vintage goods, art and crafts, with artisanal food stands, every Sunday year round from 10-5*

UPPER WEST SIDE

ATTRACTIONS

Lincoln Center for the Performing Arts (Lincoln Plaza, Columbus/w63rd)
[70 Lincoln Center Plaza] *the major cultural center of NYC and great home of the arts with the Metropolitan Opera, NY Philharmonic, Alice Tully Hall, Juilliard School, NYC Ballet, Jazz at Lincoln Center & Film at Lincoln Center, can get tickets online*

New York Historical Society Museum & Library (museum dedicated to the history of New York City, CentralPkWest/w77th)
[170 Central Park West] *Founded in 1804 as NYC's first museum, it is dedicated to presenting art, artifacts and exhibitions focusing on history of the city of New York. Can buy tickets in-person/online. Admission is pay-as-you-wish from 6-8 pm on Fridays*

Beacon Theatre (concert music hall, Broadway/w74th)
[2124 Broadway] *famous 1920's UWS concert hall and opulent theater with exquisite detailing, balcony seating & superior acoustics. Still a destination spot for headline musicians & entertainers*

American Museum of Natural History (science and history museum w/dinosaurs & planetariums, CentralPkWest/w77-81st)
[200 Central Park West] *science and history museum that's the place to see everything about our natural history, often in cool dioramas that recreate their settings - early man, dinosaurs, ocean creatures w/Rose Center for Earth & Space, Hayden Planetarium, museum cafe, can get tickets online, pay-what-you wish admission is available to all NY, NJ and CT residents with ID's online.*

Rose Center for Earth & Space (planetarium, CentralPkWest/w77th)
[200 Central Park West] *Rose Center for Earth & Space houses the Hayden Planetarium within the American Museum of Natural History complex, the planetarium has a 67 ft dome screen that encloses you in an all-encompassing space environment to see narrated films about the stars, galaxies and outer space, can get tickets online, pay-what-you wish admission is available to all NY, NJ and CT residents with ID's online.*

Central Park (grand city park of NYC, w59th/Central Pk thru w110th/5th)
[59th St to 110th St, 5th Ave to Central Park W] *one of the most famous parks in the world, Central Park is a grand, magnificent and very designed swath of nature right in the middle of the city. A masterpiece of landscape architecture and urban planning created over 150 years ago by Frederick Law Olmstead & Calvert Vaux.*
It spans 51 blocks from 59th St to 110th St along Fifth Avenue. Lots to do in the park but most of all, it's a nice walk on a beautiful day, free park Wifi

UPPER EAST SIDE

quick directions
Take 4, 5, 6 train uptown to 86th St Lexington Ave stop [e86th/Lex]

COFFEE

Oslo Coffee Roasters (coffee shop, e75th/1st near York Ave)
[422 E 75th St] *Brooklyn-based coffee roaster in a small low-key, cozy cafe interior with pastries, cold brews, cortados, limited bench seating, grab & go (no Wifi, no bathroom)*

Birch Coffee (coffee shop, e62nd/Lex)
[134 1/2 E 62nd St] *tiny hole-in-the-wall outpost of Birch coffee, pastries w/limited seating, grab & go (no Wifi, no bathroom)*

Ralph's Coffee (fancy coffee stand in front of Ralph Lauren store, Madison/e72nd)
[888 Madison Ave] *posh coffee stand in lobby of Ralph Lauren store serving coffee, lattes & tea with pastries, desserts, afternoon sandwich specials, some seating inside but more for patio seating in front, near the Frick Museum, Wifi (bathrooms in store)*

Bluestone Lane (coffee shop, near Met & Guggenheim museum, 5th/e90th)
[1085 5th Ave] *Aussie-inspired coffee chain, pastries and food, big on avocado toast, in arched church space on 5th Ave - this location has seating booths within nooks of the church architecture, also outside patio seating during nice weather (no Wifi)*

UPPER EAST SIDE

Starbucks (coffee shop near Met Museum, Madison/e84th)
[1142 Madison Ave] *formerly a Starbucks Reserve bar with specialty coffees so it's a roomy store for uptown w/lounge chair seating & comfy interior space, Wifi*

TEA

Alice's Tea Cup Chapter II (tea room, famous scones, e64th/Lex)
[156 E 64th St] *tea room & breakfast place, cozy spot for a tea get-together, famous for its scones and its Alice in Wonderland theme w/tea drinks, breakfast, sandwiches, pastries & whimsical decor*

Kings' Carriage House (tea room, affordable tea set specials, e82nd/2nd)
[251 E 82nd St] *reasonably priced tea sets in UES duplex serving classic afternoon high tea in English country-house décor w/sandwiches, pastries & pots of tea*

Vivi Bubble Tea (bubble tea shop, 2nd/e82nd)
[1324 2nd Ave] *small bubble tea spot serving bubble teas, milk teas, fruit teas & lemonade teas with snacks*

EATS

($)
Bagelworks (bagel shop, breakfast sandwiches, made on premises, 1stAve/e66th)
[1229 1st Ave] *classic NYC bagel shop that makes its own bagels everyday on premises, also has breakfast sandwiches, often has lines, no seating, well regarded, grab & go*

Katagiri (Japanese groceries/eats, e59th/3rd)
[224 E 59th St] *est. 1907, says it's "The oldest Japanese grocery store in the USA" - sushi, rice balls, prepared bento boxes & groceries, a few seats in front, more grab & go*

Xi'an Famous Foods (Chinese noodle house, e78th/2nd)
[328 E 78th St] *NYC chain of western Chinese cuisine with spicy, hand-ripped noodle dishes, larger space w/seating*

Dos Toros Taqueria (burrito, tacos, Lex/e77th)
[1111 Lexington Ave] *fast casual chain of SF Taqueria w/mission style build-your-own burritos, tacos, quesadilla, burrito bowls, reliable mid-sized place w/seating*

($$)

JG Melon (classic NY place, famous cheeseburger, 3rd/e74th)
[1291 3rd Ave] *classic old school NYC restaurant & bar famous for its simple cheeseburger, served w/crispy waffle-cut fries, cash only!*

The Penrose (upscale gastropub w/comfort food, 2ndAve/e83rd)
[1590 2nd Ave] *upscale gastropub with American comfort food, warm rustic interior, serves picture-perfect comfort food and cocktails, often crowded at brunch, popular*

Orwasher's Artisan Bakery (sandwiches, jelly donuts, e78th/2nd)
[308 E 78th St] *artisan bakery, popular for its fresh baked hand-filled jelly donuts, makes breads, croissants & muffins, well regarded, no seating, grab & go*

Schaller's Stube Sausage Bar (German sausages, bratwurst, 2ndAve/e86th)
[1654 2nd Ave] *German sausage & hot dog place that uses high-quality wurst meats, sauerkraut, bratwurst, brioche buns w/limited seating in back, more grab & go*

The Jeffrey Craft Beer & Bites (beer garden, near tram & bridge, e60th/2nd)
[311 E 60th St] *laid back craft beer and food hideaway with festive backyard space, large craft beer selection in a relaxed & warm wood brick setting w/late night happy hour specials, good meetup spot in this part of town by the Queensboro Bridge*

Shake Shack - Upper East Side (burger place, e86th/Lex)
[152 E 86th St] *popular NYC burger chain, often on best burger lists w/seating in this basement level restaurant branch, can get crowded since on a busy street*

Dig (farm fresh marketbowl, Lex/e87)
[1297 Lexington Ave] *fast casual food chain, serves farm-fresh market bowl with comfort food, larger-store place w/seating, reliable go-to option*

($$$)

Jones Woods Foundry (British gastropub, comfort food, e76th/1stAve)
[401 E 76th St] *fancy British gastropub with fish & chips along with magazine-style English comfort food on the upscale British side - scotch eggs, bangers & mash, shepherd's pie & yorkshire pudding w/outdoor patio area during warmer months*

Café Sabarsky (Austrian restaurant & cafe at the Neue Galerie art museum, can enter separately from museum, 5th/e86th)
[1048 5th Ave] *ritzy cafe in art museum inspired by old Vienna cafes serving signature Viennese desserts like apple strudels, chocolate mousse cakes, sausage dishes and savory plates, open to public at breakfast & brunch on a first serve basis, reservations better*

UPPER EAST SIDE

Tanoshi Sushi Sake Bar (Japanese sushi restaurant, York/e73rd)
[1372 York Ave] *highly-rated Japanese sushi in a much more casual setting, omakase special is said to be less expensive than what's charged in fancier big-name places*

($$$$)

Sushi of Gari UES (fancy highly-rated sushi, e78th/1st)
[402 E 78th St] *considered one of the top NYC fancy sushi restaurants, w/omakase special, well regarded & expensive, reservations*

Sushi Seki (fancy highly-rated sushi, 1st/e62nd)
[1143 1st Ave] *another top NYC sushi restaurant, serves omakase, well regarded & expensive, reservations*

DRINKS & BARS

($$)

Cantor Rooftop & Garden Bar at the Met (rooftop garden bar at Met museum w/fantastic city & Central Park views, part of museum admission, only open during the warm weather seasons, check museum website - metmuseum.org/visit/dining (e5th/80th)
[1000 5th Ave, Floor 5] *in the warmer months, the Met opens its Cantor Rooftop Garden with spectacular, panoramic views of the city's skyscrapers surrounding Central Park, becoming both a bustling rooftop bar scene & popular viewing place for museum-goers*

The Pony Bar (craft beer bar hangout in UES, 1st/e75th)
[1444 1st Ave] *fun hangout bar in UES focused on craft beer & pub food, set up like a woodsy inn with cask-barrel tables & planked wood all-around, has beer boards to keep track of all the Porters & IPAs they have on tap, with a full-sized canoe on the ceiling*

The Penrose (upscale gastropub w/comfort food, 2ndAve/e83rd)
[1590 2nd Ave] *upscale gastropub with American comfort food, warm rustic interior, serves picture-perfect comfort food and cocktails, often crowded at brunch, popular*

The Jeffrey Craft Beer & Bites (beer garden, near tram & bridge, e60th/2nd)
[311 E 60th St] *laid back craft beer and food hideaway with festive backyard space, large craft beer selection in a relaxed & warm wood brick setting w/late night happy hour specials, good meetup spot in this part of town by the Queensboro Bridge*

SHOPPING

Bloomingdale's (famous classic NYC department store, 3rd/59th)
[1000 3rd Ave] *iconic and energetic department store on Third Avenue that was one of New York's earliest fancy department stores, sells higher end but relatively affordable designer brands, modern to upscale clothes in a well laid-out store space*

Argosy Book Store (beloved antique & rare used book store, e59th/Lexington)
[116 E 59th St] *true book lovers destination, independent used bookstore that's considered an Upper East Side gem. Family-owned since 1925, sells everything from valuable collectors items and expensive rare editions to $1 bargains bins, good sized and well worn place specializing in old & rare books, prints, autographs, antique maps w/upstairs map shop*

Shopping at designer stores & boutiques
{Madison Ave} *designer stores & boutiques on Madison Avenue from 57th to 86th St*

FUN STUFF

Paris Theater (classic single-screen art house theater, w58th/5th)
[4 w58th St] *classy & well-maintained single-screen movie theater that's the last of its kind in Manhattan, curated for long art house or foreign movie showings, across from Plaza Hotel*

Sotheby's (auction house w/art galleries, York/e72nd)
[1334 York Ave] *Sotheby's New York auction headquarters is a place that welcomes collectors and art lovers who can view the collection in their galleries for free before it goes off to buyers for sale (can even participate if you're a big spender) Also a coat check & Sotheby's cafe to relax in*

MANHATTAN VIEWS

Cantor Rooftop & Garden Bar at the Met (rooftop garden bar at Met museum w/ fantastic city & Central Park views, part of museum admission, only open during the warm weather seasons, check museum website - metmuseum.org/visit/dining (e5th/80th)
[1000 5th Ave, Floor 5] *in the warmer months, the Met opens its Cantor Rooftop Garden with spectacular, panoramic views of the city's skyscrapers surrounding Central Park, becoming both a bustling rooftop bar scene & popular viewing place for museum-goers*

UPPER EAST SIDE

Central Park (grand city park of NYC, w59th/Central Pk thru w110th/5th) [59th St to 110th St, 5th Ave to Central Park W] *one of the most famous parks in the world, Central Park is a grand, magnificent and very designed swath of nature right in the middle of the city. A masterpiece of landscape architecture and urban planning created over 150 years ago by Frederick Law Olmstead & Calvert Vaux. It spans 51 blocks from 59th St to 110th St along Fifth Avenue. Lots to do in the park but most of all, it's a nice walk on a beautiful day, free park Wifi*

ATTRACTIONS

Metropolitan Museum of Art (biggest art museum in city, top NYC attraction, 5th/80th) [1000 5th Ave] *The Met is the top tourist attraction in NYC & biggest art museum in the city, amongst the great museums of the world housing mainly traditional art with galleries for modern, contemporary & ancient art. Always has major exhibitions on view. Night hours on Fri & Sat till 9 pm. For New York State residents (w/accepted ID) & students in NY, CT, NJ, admission is pay-what-you-wish.*

The Guggenheim Museum (art museum in Frank Lloyd Wright's famous spiral landmark building, on 5th Ave a few blocks from the Met, 5th/e88th) [1071 5th Ave] *Spiral art museum on 5th Ave that in itself is considered on of the great masterpieces of architect Frank Lloyd Wright, housing the art collection of the Peggy Guggenheim with impressionist, modern & contemporary works as well as featured exhibitions. Every Sat from 5-8pm, admission is pay-what-you-wish, better to reserve those tickets online since on-site tickets can be limited.*

Frick Museum (art museum in 5th Ave mansion, w/Vermeers, e70th/5th) [1 E 70th St] reopening in late 2024, works up at Frick Madison until March 3, 2024 *Frick collection is a museum housed in industrialist Henry Clay Frick's Fifth Ave mansion showing the old master art collection he amassed including Rembrandts, Vermeers, Whistlers & Renaissance masters. Also has serene indoor garden court with fountain, greenery and water pool*

- - -

Until March 3. 2024, see works at Frick Madison
Frick Madison, 945 Madison Ave (@e75th St)
While the main Frick Museum is closed for renovations most of 2023 & 2024, the art collection will be shown at its temporary home nearby at The Frick Madison, 945 Madison Ave (@e75th St). Reopening of the main Frick Museum on 1 E 70th St is expected sometime in late 2024. Pay-what-you-wish admission is on Thursdays from 4:00 to 6:00 p.m.

Neue Galerie (Austrian/German Expressionist art museum in UES mansion, 5th/e86th)
[1048 5th Ave] *Nue Galerie is an Upper East Side mansion converted to an art museum that primarily showcases early 20th century German and Austrian art & design, featuring artists of that era such as Gustav Klimt and Egon Schiele as well as works from the Art Nouveau, Bauhaus & Weimar Periods.*
Free admission from 6-8pm on the first Friday of the month
- - -
The Cafe Sabarsky - *Visitors can also dine inside the museum at the* **Cafe Sabarsky** *- a ritzy cafe that's inspired by the Vienna cafes of old serving signature Viennese desserts like apple strudels & chocolate mousse cakes*

Museum Mile (art museums along 5thAve between e82nd & e105th St)
[btw 82nd & 105th Streets, Fifth Ave] *stretch of Fifth Ave known as "Museum Mile" w/ major museums and art galleries (The Met, Guggenheim, Neue Galerie)*

Central Park (grand city park of NYC, w59th/Central Pk thru w110th/5th)
[59th St to 110th St, 5th Ave to Central Park W] *one of the most famous parks in the world, Central Park is a grand, magnificent and very designed swath of nature right in the middle of the city. A masterpiece of landscape architecture and urban planning created over 150 years ago by Frederick Law Olmstead & Calvert Vaux.*
It spans 51 blocks from 59th St to 110th St along Fifth Avenue. Lots to do in the park but most of all, it's a nice walk on a beautiful day, free park Wifi

Park Avenue Armory (palatial Gilded Age structure used for art exhibitions, events & tours, Park/e66th)
[643 Park Ave] *grand & palatial Gothic Revival structure from the Gilded Age with high ceilings and lush interiors that used to be a National Guard and volunteer militia armory in the late 19th century. Now those large spaces are hosting big art exhibitions, events, talks and guided tours. Visit armoryonpark.org for schedule & tickets*

Sotheby's (auction house w/art galleries, York/e72nd)
[1334 York Ave] *Sotheby's New York auction headquarters is a place that welcomes both art collectors & art lovers who can view the collection in their galleries for free before it goes off to buyers for sale. There is also a coat check & Sotheby's Cafe to relax in*

MIDTOWN
57th St - Central Park

quick directions
Take N, W, R uptown to 5th Ave/59th stop [e59th/5thAve]

COFFEE

Little Collins (Australian coffee bar & breakfast spot, 3rd/e45th)
[708 3rd Ave] *well regarded coffee place, serves Counter Culture coffee, known for its espressos, flat whites & now a destination breakfast spot, w/seating (no Wifi)*

Birch Coffee (tiny cafe, 9th/w57th)
[844 9th Ave] *tiny cafe and well-kept place serving coffee & pastries w/limited seating, grab & go (no Wifi)*

Rex (city coffee shop, 10th/w57th)
[864 10th Ave] *mid-sized rustic modern coffee shop, serves Counter Culture coffee, food, pastries & sandwiches w/tables, seating, & big windows Wifi*

TEA

Afternoon Tea at BG (fancy tea set at Bergdorf Goodman dept store, w5th/58th)
[754 5th Ave] *famous tea set special at BG restaurant on 7th floor of the upscale Bergdorf Goodman women's store, served daily 3-5 pm, pricey*

Palm Court at the Plaza (fancy tea set special at Plaza Hotel, w5th/59th)
[768 5th Ave] *fancy tea set in old New York Plaza Hotel opulence, afternoon tea daily 10:30 am - 4 pm, pricey*

EATS

($)
Katagiri (Japanese groceries/eats, e59th/3rd)
[224 E 59th St] *est. 1907, says it's "The oldest Japanese grocery store in the USA" with sushi, rice balls, prepared bento boxes & groceries, a few seats in front, more grab & go*

Whole Foods Market (lower level of Whole Foods, ColumbusCircle/w59th)
[10 Columbus Circle] *food court at the Whole Foods in lower level area of Time Waner Center, w/hot food, prepared foods, salad bar, w/seating and booths, often crowded*

($$)
Burger Joint (burger place inside Thompson Central Park NY Hotel, w56th/6th)
[119 W 56th St] *destination burger joint on top NYC burger lists, in a wood-paneled time capsule dive bar with 80's movie posters, look for neon burger sign, often crowded*

Sfilatino Italian Gourmet (Italian gourmet sandwiches, w57th/9th)
[342 W 57th St] *well regarded cafe focused on gourmet Italian sandwiches, coffee and rich desserts, wood counter and painted map interior w/seating & tables*

Urbanspace at 570 Lex (urban gourmet food hall, Lex/e51st)
[570 Lexington Ave] *urban food hall space in midtown with Bao by Kaya asian casual, Pita Yeero Greek gyros & bowls, Takumi Taco & Little Collins coffee, upstairs level for seating*

($$$)

Yakitori Totto (Japanese skewers, w55th/8th)
[251 W 55th St] *Japanese skewer restaurant in Theater district w/close quarter seating and energetic atmosphere, popular*

DRINKS & BARS

($$)

Draught 55 (craft beer hall, e55th/2nd)
[245 E 55th St] *rustic-style beer hall with inviting glass atrium, serving craft beer and well-made food in a big space w/long wood tables & patio seating area outside*

The Jeffrey Craft Beer & Bites (beer garden, near tram & bridge, e60th/2nd)
[311 E 60th St] *laid back craft beer and food hideaway with festive backyard space, large craft beer selection in a relaxed & warm wood brick setting w/late night happy hour specials, good meetup spot in this part of town by the Queensboro Bridge*

($$$)

P.J. Clarke's (old time NYC saloon bar, popular Cadillac burger, 3rd/e55th)
[915 3rd Ave] *est. 1884, old time NYC saloon bar with long history, Cadillac burger often makes top NYC lists, Frank Sinatra used to be a regular here w/his own reserved table, good happy hour*

SHOPPING

Bloomingdale's (famous classic NYC department store, 3rd/e59th)
[1000 3rd Ave] *iconic and energetic department store on Third Avenue that was one of New York's earliest fancy department stores, sells higher end but relatively affordable designer brands, modern to upscale clothes in a well laid-out store space*

Bergdorf Goodman (fancy upscale women's department store in former mansion, BG Men's store across the street, 5th/w58th)
[754 5th Ave] *upscale department store housed in the former Vanderbilt mansion facing Central Park & 5th Ave, known mainly for how expensive and high-end it is, where ladies who lunch and the 1% come to shop. BG Men's store across the street [at 745 5th Ave]*

Shopping on Fifth Avenue by 57th St (btw 50 & 60th st)
[5th Ave] *Saks Fifth Ave, Tiffany's, Bergdorf Goodman and luxury stores on 5th Ave.*

Argosy Book Store (beloved antique & rare used book store, e59th/Lexington)
[116 E 59th St] *true book lovers destination, independent used bookstore that's considered an Upper East Side gem. Family-owned since 1925, sells everything from valuable collectors items and expensive rare editions to $1 bargains bins, good sized and well worn place specializing in old & rare books, prints, autographs, antique maps w/ upstairs map shop*

54 Vintage Vinyl (small vinyl LP music shop, w54th/8th)
[246 w54th St] *small, tidy and well organized vinyl LP record store near 57th St with vintage records ranging from hip-hop, classical, rock, reggae to soundtracks*

Shops at Columbus Circle (Time Warner Center, ColumbusCrcl/w59th)
[10 Columbus Circle] *mall complex in Time Warner Center at Columbus Circle featuring shops like Williams Sonoma cookware, H&M clothing, J.Crew clothing, TUMI luggage, Jo Malone London fragrances, Alo yoga activeware, Lululemon activewear, La Maison du Chocolat, Ladurée macarons, Moleskin stationary, luxury brand stores, fancy restaurants, Jazz at Lincoln Center & a Whole Foods on the basement level*

INDOOR PUBLIC SPACES

590 Madison / Atrium at 57th Street (large indoor plaza w/atrium, Madison/e57th)
[590 Madison Ave] *enormous public plaza inside a large light-filled atrium, complete with indoor garden, patio seating, placed trees & plenty of space to relax in, coffee & snacks, Wifi*

OUTDOOR PUBLIC SPACES

Central Park (grand city park of NYC, w59th/Central Pk thru w110th/5th)
[59th St to 110th St, 5th Ave to Central Park W] *one of the most famous parks in the world, Central Park is a grand, magnificent and very designed swath of nature right in the middle of the city. A masterpiece of landscape architecture and urban planning created over 150 years ago by Frederick Law Olmstead & Calvert Vaux. It spans 51 blocks from 59th St to 110th St along Fifth Avenue. Lots to do in the park but most of all, it's a nice walk on a beautiful day, free park Wifi*

Sutton Place Park (small city park with stunning views of the East River & the Queensboro Bridge at end of 57th St , Sutton Place/e57th)
[1 Sutton Place South] *hidden park terrace at end of East 57th St with spectacular views of East River & Queensboro Bridge, often featured in movies and paintings*

FUN STUFF

Paris Theater (classic single-screen art house theater, w58th/5th)
[4 w58th St] *classy & well-maintained single-screen movie theater that's the last of its kind in Manhattan, curated for long art house or foreign movie showings, across from Plaza Hotel*

54 Vintage Vinyl (small vinyl LP music shop, w54th/8th)
[246 w54th St] *small, tidy and well organized vinyl LP record store near 57th St with vintage records ranging from hip-hop, classical, rock, reggae to soundtracks*

ATTRACTIONS

Central Park (grand city park of NYC, w59th/Central Pk thru w110th/5th)
[59th St to 110th St, 5th Ave to Central Park W] *one of the most famous parks in the world, Central Park is a grand, magnificent and very designed swath of nature right in the middle of the city. A masterpiece of landscape architecture and urban planning created over 150 years ago by Frederick Law Olmstead & Calvert Vaux. It spans 51 blocks from 59th St to 110th St along Fifth Avenue. Lots to do in the park but most of all, it's a nice walk on a beautiful day, free park Wifi*

Museum of Modern Art (MoMA, modern art museum, e53rd/5th)
[11 W 53rd St] *the big NYC art destination besides the Met w/Van Gogh's "Starry Night", showing impressionist, modern & contemporary art, can get reserved timed tickets online at website, also free admission for New York City residents on the first Friday evening of each month from 4-8 p.m, can reserve those online as well*

Shopping on Fifth Avenue by 57th St (btw 50 & 60th st)
[5th Ave] *Saks Fifth Ave, Tiffany's, Bergdorf Goodman and luxury stores on 5th Ave*

MIDTOWN
5th Avenue - Midtown East

quick directions
Take B, D, F, M uptown to 47-50 Sts Rockefeller Ctr stop [w48th/6thAve]

COFFEE

Little Collins (Australian coffee bar & breakfast spot, 3rd/e45th)
[708 3rd Ave] *well regarded coffee place, serves Counter Culture coffee, known for its espressos, flat whites & now a destination breakfast spot, w/seating (no Wifi)*

Starbucks (coffee shop in food court below Rockefeller Plaza, w49th/5th)
[30 Rockefeller Plz] *centrally located Starbucks with a generous amount of cafe seating and activity in main area of the food court below Rockefeller Plaza, Wifi*

Blue Bottle Coffee (coffee shop in food court below Rockefeller Plaza, w49th/5th)
[30 Rockefeller Plz] *SF coffee roaster chain, pour over coffee w/limited seating, Wifi*

Maman (gourmet French American cafe & bakery, w48th/5th)
[12 W 48th St] *stylish French American cafe with an elegant gourmet aesthetic, breakfast, brunch, bakery w/tables & seating in long space near Rockefeller Center (no Wifi)*

TEA

Afternoon Tea at BG (fancy tea set at Bergdorf Goodman dept store, w5th/58th)
[754 5th Ave] *famous tea set special at BG restaurant on 7th floor of the upscale Bergdorf Goodman women's store, served daily 3-5 pm, pricey*

Palm Court at the Plaza (fancy tea set special at Plaza Hotel, w5th/59th)
[768 5th Ave] *fancy tea set in old New York Plaza Hotel opulence, afternoon tea daily 10:30 am - 4 pm, pricey*

Cha Cha Matcha - Bryant Park (matcha latte shop near Bryant Park, 5th/e42nd)
[501 5th Ave] *matcha latte shop near Bryant Park with matcha drinks, chai tea & soft serve ice cream, some seating, more grab & go*

EATS

($)

Katagiri - Grand Central (Japanese grocery/eats, Lex/e41st)
[370 Lexington Ave] *well regarded Japanese grocery store near Grand Central with rice balls, sushi, prepared foods, w/limited seating & a ramen eat-in area*

Dos Toros Taqueria (Mexican food, burritos, tacos, Lex/45th)
[465 Lexington Ave] *fast casual chain of SF taqueria, mission style build-your-own burritos, tacos, quesadilla, burrito bowls, good-size place w/seating, reliable*

Dos Toros Taqueria (Mexican food, burritos, tacos, w52nd/5th)
[52 W 52nd St] *fast casual chain of SF taqueria, mission style build-your-own burritos, tacos, quesadilla, burrito bowls, good-size place w/seating, reliable*

($$)

Ippudo 5th Ave (Japanese ramen, w46th/5th)
[24 W 46th St] *popular Japanese ramen shop with a good reputation in NYC, focused on gourmet ramen bowls w/comfort foods in an orderly restaurant space, reliable place in this part of midtown with less affordable options for dining out*

Urbanspace at 570 Lex (urban gourmet food hall, Lex/e51st)
[570 Lexington Ave] *urban food hall space in midtown with Bao by Kaya asian casual, Pita Yeero Greek gyros & bowls, Takumi Taco & Little Collins coffee, upstairs level for seating*

Rockefeller Center (food court below Rockefeller Plaza, 5th/w50th)
[30 Rockefeller Plaza] *food court & stores below Rockefeller Plaza - Alidoro sandwiches, Magnolia Bakery, Dough donuts, Bill's Bar & Burger, Blue Ribbon sushi bar, Blue Bottle coffee & large Starbucks coffee area w/seating, tables & Wifi*

Bill's Bar & Burger (burger restaurant, Rockefeller Center, 5th/51st)
[16 West 51st St] *well known burger restaurant in midtown, solid and affordable place with American comfort food w/seating & tables, good for groups*

DRINKS & BARS

($$)

Whiskey Trader (triple-decker sports pub & lounge, w55th/6th)
[71 W 55th St] *casual sports/after-work bar in heart of midtown with a tri-level wooden pub, barreled interior, cozy couches & lounge section, no food but free popcorn, can get crowded*

($$$)

Valerie (fancy art deco cocktail bar w/upscale comfort food, w45th/5th)
[45 W 45th St] *glamorous space inside that looks like a 1920's Art Deco movie set with a cocktail bar, gourmet comfort food & festive atmosphere*

Le Chalet (cocktail bar/wooden lodge-lounge inside Saks 5th Avenue, 50th/5th)
[8 E 50th St, inside Saks 5th Ave] *accessible by a curved staircase below L'Avenue at Saks restaurant, travel down to an intimate wood-paneled lounge set up like a dimly-lit hunting lodge with couches, armchairs and sofa lamps, serving cocktails & drinks*

SHOPPING

5th Avenue shopping
[5th Ave] *clothing, designer & luxury brands as well as famous department stores along 5th Avenue - Saks Fifth Avenue, Bergdorf Goodman, Tiffany's*

Saks Fifth Avenue (fancy dept store across from Rockefeller Center, 5th/e49th)
[611 5th Ave] *one of the classic NYC big department stores across from Rockefeller Center with expensive, high-end clothes & accessories. Saks Fifth Avenue was originally created as a "dream store" by the retail store owners Horace Saks & Bernard Gimbel in the 1920's. Their idea was to combine their stores downtown into this large 10-story super structure of a department store uptown. It still stands today as a premiere NYC shopping destination*

Bergdorf Goodman (fancy upscale women's department store in former mansion, BG Men's store across the street, 5th/w58th)
[754 5th Ave] *upscale department store housed in the former Vanderbilt mansion facing Central Park & 5th Ave, known mainly for how expensive and high-end it is, where ladies who lunch and the 1% come to shop. BG Men's store across the street [at 745 5th Ave]*

Muji Fifth Avenue (Japanese items, clothes, 5th/e41st)
[475 5th Ave] *Muji flagship NYC store w/Japanese office & art supplies, house items, fragrances and clothing with tasteful and elegant products*

Uniqlo 5th Ave (Japanese clothing, flagship NY store, 5th/w53rd)
[666 5th Ave] *flagship NYC store on 5th Avenue, major clothing brand in Japan, affordable, stylish clothes that are well designed and popular*

Apple Fifth Avenue (flagship NY store of Apple computer, 5th/e59th)
[767 5th Ave] *massive and sleek flagship NY Apple store underneath plaza marked by the luminous Apple glass cube structure above it, on 5th Ave across from Central Park*

INDOOR PUBLIC SPACES

590 Madison / Atrium at 57th Street (large indoor plaza w/atrium, Madison/e57th)
[590 Madison Ave] *enormous public plaza inside a large light-filled atrium, complete with indoor garden, patio seating, placed trees & plenty of space to relax in, coffee & snacks, Wifi*

Park Avenue Plaza (indoor public plaza on 52nd St, e52nd/Park)
[55 E 52nd St] *indoor public plaza at office building with waterfalls, patio seating, Starbucks and with musicians playing occasionally (no Wifi)*

OUTDOOR PUBLIC SPACES

Paley Park (city park w/waterfalls, e53rd/5th)
[3 E 53rd St] *elegant urban park with waterfalls & outdoor patio seating, quiet place in city near 5th Ave, closed on weekends (*may be temporarily closed for rennovations in 2024)*

Greenacre Park (city park w/waterfalls, e51st/3rd)
[217 E 51st St] *hidden gem of a park in the heart of midtown with waterfalls, patio seating and nature to relax in this oasis from the city outside*

NY Public Library Terrace (outdoor terrace plaza in front of library, 5th/e41st)
[476 5th Ave] *elegant terrace in front plaza area of library by the lions. elevated over 5th Ave w/plenty of patio seating - great place for lunch, meeting up, people watching or reading a book*

FUN STUFF

Paris Theater (classic single-screen art house theater, w58th/5th)
[4 w58th St] *classy & well-maintained single-screen movie theater that's the last of its kind in Manhattan, curated for long art house or foreign movie showings, across from Plaza Hotel*

ATTRACTIONS

5th Avenue shopping
[5th Ave] *clothing, designer & luxury brands as well as famous department stores along 5th Avenue - Saks Fifth Avenue, Bergdorf Goodman, Tiffany's*

Rockefeller Center (art deco city plaza, major attraction, 5th/w50th)
[30 Rockefeller Plz] *a top NYC tourist destination, the plaza, building and stores, iconic ice rink opens in winter w/dining concourse, large Starbucks & Wifi downstairs*

St. Patrick's Cathedral (gothic cathedral church on 5th Ave, e51st/5th)
[14 E 51st St] *grand gothic cathedral church of NYC on 5th Ave with towering spires and dazzling architecture, often crowded with tourists, free*

New York Public Library (grand NYC library, w/lions, 5th/e41st)
[476 5th Ave] *glorious, opulent NYC library with its iconic lions at the entrance to research or study in grandeur, Rose Reading Room, exhibitions, rooftop terrace, next to Bryant Park, Wifi*

Museum of Modern Art (MoMA, modern art museum, e53rd/5th)
[11 W 53rd St] *the big NYC art destination besides the Met w/Van Gogh's "Starry Night", showing impressionist, modern & contemporary art, can get reserved timed tickets online at website, also free admission for New York City residents on the first Friday evening of each month from 4-8 p.m, can reserve those online as well*

Christie's New York (auction house w/art galleries, next to Rockefeller Plaza, w49th/5th)
[20 Rockefeller Plaza] *world famous auction house, where public can browse the art collections up for auction in their galleries, open to public & free*

MIDTOWN
Grand Central - 42nd St

quick directions
Take 4, 5, 6, 7 uptown to Grand Central Station stop [e42nd/ParkAve]

COFFEE

Perk Kafe (neighborhood coffee shop in Murray Hill area, e37th/Lex)
[162 E 37th St] *quirky neighborhood cafe in Murray Hill area, serving Stumptown coffee in a cozy setting with a big, thick wood table w/seating, Wifi*

Lucid Cafe (neighborhood cafe, Lex/e38th)
[311 Lexington Ave] *laid back, quaint neighborhood cafe in a small cozy space with limited seating (no Wifi, no bathroom)*

Blue Bottle Coffee (small coffee shop near Grand Central, e42nd/Madison)
[60 E 42nd St] *SF coffee roaster chain, pour over, small shop next to Grand Central, w/few seats, little seating, grab & go (no Wifi, no bathroom)*

Bluestone Lane (coffee shop, e47th/Madison)
[400 Madison Ave] *Australian-inspired coffee chain with coffee and food, big on avocado toast, little seating, just grab & go (no Wifi, no bathroom)*

TEA

Cha Cha Matcha - Bryant Park (matcha latte shop near Bryant Park, 5th/e42nd)
[501 5th Ave] *matcha latte shop near Bryant Park with matcha drinks, chai tea & soft serve ice cream, some seating, more grab & go*

Gong Cha (Taiwanese bubble tea shop, w38th/6th)
[75 W 38th St] *Taiwanese bubble tea chain in mid-sized shop w/tables & seating serving bubble teas, flavored milk teas & boba teas*

EATS

($)

Katagiri - Grand Central (Japanese grocery/eats, Lex/e41st)
[370 Lexington Ave] *well regarded Japanese grocery store near Grand Central with rice balls, sushi, prepared foods, w/limited seating & a ramen eat-in area*

Dos Toros Taqueria (Mexican food, burritos, tacos, Lex/e45th)
[465 Lexington Ave] *fast casual chain of SF taqueria, mission style build-your-own burritos, tacos, quesadilla, burrito bowls, mid-size place w/seating, reliable*

Café Zaiya in Kinokuniya (Japanese cafe in bookstore, 2nd fl, 6th/e41st)
[1073 6th Ave] *cafe on 2nd floor of Japanese bookstore w/prepared Japanese foods, coffee, pastries, has table seating & counter views of Bryant Park & Midtown*

($$)

Alidoro - Bryant Park (Italian sandwich shop, e39th/Madison)
[18 E 39th St] *authentic Italian gourmet sandwiches, midtown branch of highly regarded Soho sandwich shop w/seating in a lofty stylish interior*

Urbanspace Vanderbilt Food Hall (urban gourmet food hall, Park/e45th)
[230 Park Ave] *urban food hall behind Grand Central w/Bash Burger, Kuro-Obi ramen, Mian Kitchen modern Taiwanese, La Palapa Taco bar, Dough donuts & Moka Matcha located behind Grand Central - take escalator up from GC main floor to hallway going to 45th St*

Grand Central Dining Concourse (food court, dining in basement level of Grand Central Station, e42nd/Park)
[89 E 42nd St] *downstairs main food court of Grand Central Station w/Shake Shack, Grand Central Oyster Bar, Luke's Lobster, Doughnut Plant & Grand Central Mkt upstairs*

Shake Shack - Grand Central (burger place at Grand Central Dining, e42nd/Park)
[89 E 42nd St] *popular NYC burger chain that's often on best burger lists, the location downstairs at Grand Central has its own seating area within the dining concourse*

Shake Shack - Midtown East (burger place, few blocks from Grand Central, e40th/3rd)
[600 3rd Ave] *popular NYC burger chain, often on best burger lists, in a less crowded spot a few blocks from Grand Central with a small outdoor plaza next to it*

Luke's Lobster Midtown East (lobster shack, lobster rolls, e43rd/3rd)
[207 E 43rd St] *Maine Lobster rolls, crabs, seafood shack w/seating & outdoor courtyard*

($$$$)

Sushi Yasuda (fancy, top sushi, e43rd/3rd)
[204 E 43rd St] *a top NYC sushi restaurant, Michelin-rated & highly regarded, reservations*

DRINKS & BARS

($$)

The Shakespeare (British gastropub in basement of William Hotel, e39th/Park)
[24 E 39th St] *atmospheric British gastropub in William hotel w/fish & chips, scotch eggs & British pub food in a rustic-styled setting that evokes a Shakespearean era tavern*

Stout NYC (after-work alehouse & pub bar near Grand Central, e41st/Park)
[60 E 41st St] *alehouse bar with popular happy hour for after-work crowd w/draughts, ales & standard pub fare, festive scene in a two-level, wood lodge-tyled interior*

($$$)

The Campbell ('secret' fancy bar in Grand Central/15 Vanderbilt Ave)
[15 Vanderbilt Ave] *upscale old world NY cocktail bar in a 1920's era hideaway above Grand Central, classy gilded age retreat to have a mixed drink*

The Raines Law Room at the William (fancy cocktail bar in William hotel, e39th/Park)
[24 E 39th St] *speakeasy fancy cocktail lounge inside the William Hotel, posh & dimly lit with old world elegance in separate rooms with different decor, pricey*

SHOPPING

Apple Store Grand Central (elegant Apple store on upstairs level above Grand Central Station, e42nd/Park)
[Terminal, 45 Grand Central, upstairs] *elegant Apple store that is well-cut, roomy and easy to navigate, seamlessly placed in a grand space upstairs on the upper level, looking down onto the main floor of Grand Central Station, w/Wifi*

Shopping in Grand Central Station
[Grand Central Station] *stores and shops within its corridors and entrances with an elegant Apple store on upper level plaza, w/gourmet food shopping at Grand Central Market*

INDOOR PUBLIC SPACES

New York Public Library (grand NYC library, w/lions, 5th/e41st)
[476 5th Ave] *glorious, opulent NYC library with its iconic lions at the entrance to research or study in grandeur, Rose Reading Room, exhibitions, rooftop terrace, next to Bryant Park, Wifi*

OUTDOOR PUBLIC SPACES

Bryant Park (grand city park of Midtown, great NYC park, w42nd/6th)
[E 42nd St btw 5th/6th ave] *beautiful and elegant park in heart of midtown surrounded by grand views of city, w/patio table seating, open lawns, water fountain, eats, events & park Wifi*

New York Public Library (grand NYC library, w/lions, 5th/e41st)
[476 5th Ave] *glorious, opulent NYC library with its iconic lions at the entrance to research or study in grandeur, Rose Reading Room, exhibitions, rooftop terrace, next to Bryant Park, Wifi*

Tudor City Greens Park (city parks, TudorCityPlace/e42nd)
[Tudor City Pl] *hidden gem on 42nd St, small parks up on Tudor City Greens w/walk-up park area & peaceful nature enclave with gardens, few blocks from Grand Central*

Dag Hammarskjöld Plaza (long stretch of park and plaza near the United Nations, w/one of the best NYC Greenmarkets every Wed 8-4, e46th/2nd)
[Dag Hammarskjöld Plaza] *long plaza that spans a city block with benches. trees, dog walking, events & the one of best mid-sized Greenmarkets every Wed, 8-4 p year round*

FUN STUFF

Midtown Comics Grand Central (comic books, graphic novels, Lex/e45th)
[459 Lexington Ave] *Grand Central branch of Midtown Comics - the big comics chain of Manhattan, near Grand Central on a 2nd floor walk-up store*

ATTRACTIONS

Grand Central Station (NYC's grand train station , e42nd/Park)
[87 E 42nd St] *world-renowned NYC train station and subway terminal with splendid architecture & a spectacular astral ceiling w/tours to explore station, dining, shopping, famously crowded*

New York Public Library (grand NYC library, w/lions, 5th/e41st)
[476 5th Ave] *glorious, opulent NYC library with its iconic lions at the entrance to research or study in grandeur, Rose Reading Room, exhibitions, rooftop terrace, next to Bryant Park, Wifi*

Bryant Park (grand city park of Midtown, great NYC park, w42nd/6th)
[E 42nd St btw 5th/6th ave] *beautiful and elegant park in heart of midtown surrounded by grand views of city, w/patio table seating, open lawns, water fountain, eats, events & park Wifi*

Chrysler Building (famous art deco building, Lex/e42nd)
[405 Lexington Ave] *iconic art deco NYC skyscraper and architectural masterpiece on 42nd St, more for looking at from the outside, can only visit lobby*

MIDTOWN
Times Square - Theater District

quick directions
Take 1, 2, 3, 4, 5, 6, 7 uptown to Times Sq - 42 St stop [w42nd/Broadway]

COFFEE

Starbucks Reserve Times Square (Starbucks deluxe roastery, Broadway/w47th)
[1585 Broadway] *centrally located Starbucks in Times Square w/displays & machines all around showcasing the franchise, not much seating, more of a stand-up area, Wifi (no bathroom)*

For Five Coffee Times Square (modern coffee house w/pastries, w46th/7th)
[117 W 46th St] *long modern space cafe close to Times Square w/counter and table seating, serves pastries & their signature chunky-thick cookies, Wifi (no bathrooms)*

Bluestone Lane (coffee shop in plaza, near Bryant Park, 6th/w43rd)
[1120 6th Ave] *Aussie-inspired coffee chain with coffee and food that's big on avocado toast, outpost shop on plaza w/limited seating & patio tables outside (no Wifi)*

Maman (gourmet French American cafe & bakery, w41st/6th)
[114 W 41st St] *stylish French American cafe with an elegant gourmet aesthetic, breakfast, brunch, bakery w/tables & seating, close to Bryant Park (no Wifi)*

Blue Bottle Coffee (coffee bar near Bryant Park, w40th/6th)
[54 W 40th St] *SF coffee roaster chain, feature pour over coffee, just a few seats, more for grab & go, next to Bryant Park that has patio seating outside (no Wifi)*

La Colombe Coffee Roasters - Bryant Park (coffee shop near Bryant Park, 6th/w40th)
[1045 6th Ave] *upscale stylish coffee chain in a big space w/seating, near Bryant park (no Wifi)*

Bluestone Lane Times Square (coffee shop in plaza, near Bryant Park, 8h/w42nd)
[11 Times Square] *Aussie-inspired coffee chain with coffee & food, big on avocado toast, in Times Square outpost more set up for grab & go (no Wifi)*

TEA

Bibble & Sip Bakery Cafe (Asian bakery cafe, w51st/8th)
[253 W 51st St] *mid-sized bakery cafe w/seating, serves matcha pastries, cream puffs, matcha lattes, croissants - all made in-house, well regarded, Wifi*

Angelina Paris Bryant Park (fancy French tea set & dessert cafe, 6th/w40th)
[1050 6th Ave] *stylish French dessert cafe with its signature hot chocolate & Mont Blanc dessert as well as tea time rooms for afternoon tea sets and desserts in high French style, surrounded by Rococo décor with paneled murals & mirrored walls*

EATS

($)

Los Tacos No.1 (Mexican tacos in Times Square, popular & highly rated, w43th/7th)
[229 W 43rd St] *authentic Mexican tacos in Times Sq. at original location, always highly rated on best of NYC lists, bustling with crowds at standing tables, fun NYC experience, inexpensive*

Café Zaiya in Kinokuniya (Japanese cafe in bookstore, 2nd fl, 6th/e41st)
[1073 6th Ave] *cafe on 2nd floor of Japanese bookstore w/prepared Japanese foods, coffee, pastries, has table seating & counter views of Bryant Park & Midtown*

Margon (Cuban sandwiches, 46th/7th)
[136 W 46th St] *Cuban specialties, sandwiches, rice dishes, stews, w/diner seating, well regarded sandwich place*

Empanada Mama - Hell's Kitchen (empanadas, 9thAve/w51st)
[765 9th Ave] *Latin focused food specializing in empanadas in narrow restaurant space w/seating, popular*

2 Bros Pizza (famous for reliable, no-frills cheap NYC dollar slice, 9th/w40th)
[542 9th Ave] *family-owned pizzeria that is known for being the go-to $1.50 slice shop for decent New York pizza - no frills, no fanciness, just deals, 2 slices & can of soda for $3.99*

Bibble & Sip Bakery Cafe (Asian bakery cafe, w51st/8th)
[253 W 51st St] *mid-sized bakery cafe w/seating, serves matcha pastries, cream puffs, matcha lattes, croissants - all made in-house, well regarded, Wifi*

7th St Burger Times Square (smash burger place near Times Square, 7th/w37th)
[485 7th Ave] *NYC cheeseburger chain that's gotten popular in the city with its affordable Smash Burger, fries & simple menu, mid-size place w/table & window seating*

($$)

Shake Shack - Theater District (burger place at Time Square, 8th/w44th)
[691 8th Ave] *popular NYC burger chain that's often on best NYC burger lists, since it's Times Sq, it's usually very crowded w/some seating but mostly standing tables*

Totto Ramen Hell's Kitchen (Japanese ramen, w51st/8th)
[464 W 51st St] *authentic Japanese ramen spot in theater district, highly rated and well regarded w/close quarter seating, usually has lines, popular*

Sushi Lab Rooftop NYC (stylish & affordable Japanese rooftop sushi bar at the Sanctuary Hotel, w47th/6th)
[132 W 47th St] *affordable Japanese sushi bar in rooftop space atop the Sanctuary Hotel in heart of Midtown, inviting décor with floral leafy aesthetics & lanterns in a warm open-wooded patio environment, serving hand rolls, omakase specials & seafood dishes*

Ootoya Times Square (Japanese restaurant, w41st/Broadway)
[141 W 41st St] *chain from Japan with authentic Japanese comfort food, pork cutlet, chirashi bowl, roomy, has a no tipping custom, popular in Theater district*

The Meatball Shop - Hell's Kitchen (gourmet meatballs, 9th/w53rd)
[798 9th Ave] *NYC chain of restaurants specializing in gourmet quality meatballs and comfort food, popular*

Alidoro - Bryant Park (Italian sandwich shop, e39th/Madison)
[18 E 39th St] *authentic Italian gourmet sandwiches in fancy midtown branch of the highly regarded Soho sandwich shop w/seating in a lofty stylish interior*

Whole Foods Market at Bryant Park (food hall upstairs, 6th/w41st)
[1095 Ave of Americas] *upstairs fancy gourmet food hall at centrally located Whole Foods in Midtown w/seating, tables and views of Bryant Park & Midtown*

DRINKS & BARS

($)

Jimmy's Corner (beloved Times Square dive bar, e44th/6th)
[140 W 44th St] *beloved Times Sq dive bar that's set up train carriage-style, covered with mirrors, boxing pictures and a jukebox, usually open late*

($$)

The Rum House (old time cocktail bar in Times Sq, 46th/7th)
[228 W 47th St] *cocktail and piano bar in middle of Times Sq, has live jazz & swing music with popular happy hour*

Sushi Lab Rooftop NYC (stylish & affordable Japanese rooftop sushi bar at the Sanctuary Hotel, w47th/6th)
[132 W 47th St] *affordable Japanese sushi bar in rooftop space atop the Sanctuary Hotel in heart of Midtown, inviting décor with floral leafy aesthetics & lanterns in a warm open-wooded patio environment, serving hand rolls, omakase specials & seafood dishes*

($$$)

Haven Rooftop (glass covered rooftop bar atop Sanctuary Hotel, 46th/7th)
[132 W 47th St] *smart looking rooftop bar lounge with an Aspen Lodge décor atop the Sanctuary Hotel, has comfy wood tables, couches & bricked-in nooks for cocktails, comfort food and Manhattan views under a heated glass roof*

SHOPPING

Book-Off (Japanese used bookstore w/books, cds, dvds, games, w45st/6th)
[49 W 45th St] *a cool Japanese used bookstore chain in NYC, sells English and Japanese books, music, games, dvds, electronics, manga & comics w/$1, $2 & $2.50 specials*

Kinokuniya Bookstore New York (Japanese bookstore w/cafe by Bryant Park, 6th/w41st)
[1073 6th Ave] *Japanese bookstore by Bryant Park that sells English and Japanese books, manga, comics, anime toys, art and office supplies located in basement, with the Cafe Zaiya on 2nd floor, a Japanese bakery cafe w/seating & park views*

Muji Times Square (Japanese items, clothes, near Times Sq, 8th/e40th)
[620 8th Ave] *Japanese clothing & house items store with tasteful and elegant products, office and art supplies, leans towards minimalist design w/tan & mute colors*

Shopping around Times Square
[timessquarenyc.org] *directory of stores around Times Sq scattered throughout the area*

INDOOR PUBLIC SPACES

Urban Garden Room at One Bryant Park (indoor public space, 6th/w43rd)
[One Bryant Park] *urban indoor garden space btw Times Sq & Bryant Pk, serene spot in midtown w/light-filled atrium, seating & patio tables, next to Starbucks (no Wifi)*

OUTDOOR PUBLIC SPACES

Times Square (street plazas around Times Sq w/seating, w42nd/Broadway)
[Time Square, @ 1475 Broadway] *world famous top attraction in NYC, city center of activity w/spectacular views of towering neon signs & buildings, patio seating & bustling crowds*

Bryant Park (grand city park of Midtown, great NYC park, w42nd/6th)
[E 42nd St btw 5th/6th ave] *beautiful and elegant park in heart of midtown surrounded by grand views of city, w/patio table seating, open lawns, water fountain, eats, events & park Wifi*

NY Public Library Terrace (outdoor terrace plaza in front of library, 5th/e41st)
[476 5th Ave] *elegant front plaza terrace area of library by the lions. elevated over 5th Ave w/ plenty of patio seating - great place for lunch, meeting up, people watching or reading a book*

FUN STUFF

Broadway Shows & Theaters
[Times Sq] *buy tickets at TKTS booth in Times Sq for same day shows, often at a discount*

TKTS booth in Times Square (get same-day show tickets here, Broadway/w47th)
[Times Sq] *buy same-day Broadway show tickets here in Times Square, located underneath red steps at Father Duffy Square, intersection of Broadway & 7th Ave at 47th St*

AMC Empire 25 (big movie theater in Times Sq, w42nd/8th)
[234 W 42nd St] *big AMC movie theater multiplex on 42nd St, solid reliable theater playing new movies & w/IMAX, also has Blade Runner-like views upstairs of Times Sq*

Regal E-Walk Cinemas (movie theater in Times Sq, w42nd/8th)
[247 W. 42nd St.] *big movie theater multiplex at 42nd St, across street from AMC theater, solid multiplex playing newly released movies w/RPX (IMAX-like big screen)*

Midtown Comics Times Square (comic books, graphic novels, toys, w40th/7th)
[200 W 40th St] *flagship store of Midtown comics, the big comics store of Manhattan*

ATTRACTIONS

Times Square (street plazas around Times Sq w/seating, w42nd/Broadway)
[Time Square, @ 1475 Broadway] *world famous top attraction in NYC, city center of activity w/spectacular views of towering neon signs & buildings, patio seating & bustling crowds*

Broadway Shows & Theaters
[Times Sq] *buy tickets at TKTS booth in Times Sq for same day shows, often at a discount*

TKTS booth in Times Square (get same-day show tickets here, Broadway/w47th)
[Times Sq] *buy same-day Broadway show tickets here in Times Square, located underneath red steps at Father Duffy Square, intersection of Broadway & 7th Ave at 47th St*

Radio City Music Hall (art deco concert hall, 6th/w50th)
[1260 6th Ave] *world famous art deco landmark theater of NYC, behind Rockefeller Center on 6th Ave, features The Rockettes, music concerts, shows & events*

Bryant Park (grand city park of Midtown, great NYC park, w42nd/6th)
[E 42nd St btw 5th/6th ave] *beautiful and elegant park in heart of midtown surrounded by grand views of city, w/patio table seating, open lawns, water fountain, eats, events & park Wifi*

MIDTOWN
Midtown West & Hudson Yards

quick directions
Take 7 uptown to 34th St Hudson Yards [w34th/11thAve]

COFFEE

Bird & Branch (coffee shop, w45th/9th)
[359 W 45th St] *nicely laid-out offee shop with a nature theme, matcha lattes, yogurt cups, pastries w/limited seating, Wifi (no bathroom)*

The Jolly Goat Coffee Bar (small cafe, w47th/10th)
[515 W 47th St] *small neighborhood cafe, serves Stumptown coffee with limited seating, grab & go, Wifi (no bathroom)*

Rex (coffee shop, 10th/w57th)
[864 10th Ave] *mid-sized rustic modern coffee shop, serves Counter Culture coffee, food, pastries and sandwiches w/tables, big windows & seating, Wifi*

Daily Provisions Manhattan West (gourmet cafe, 10th/w33rd)
[440 W 33rd St, Suite 90] *good-sized cafe & bakery by restauranteur who started Shake Shack, gourmet coffee, pastries, cookies, breakfast & comfort foods w/sidewalk seating, Wifi*

Birch Coffee (tiny cafe, 9thave/w57th)
[844 9th Ave] *tiny & well-kept cafe serving coffee, pastries w/limited seating, grab & go (no Wifi)*

TEA

Bibble & Sip Bakery Cafe (Asian bakery cafe, w51st/8th)
[253 W 51st St] *mid-sized bakery cafe w/seating, serves matcha pastries, cream puffs, matcha lattes, croissants - all made in-house, well regarded, Wifi*

Matchaful Cafe (matcha cafe stand inside Whole Foods, w33rd/10th)
[450 W 33rd St] *matcha latte cafe & vegan matcha soft serve stand inside Whole Foods, also serves chai lattes, teas, pastries and desserts*

High Tea Room at the Parisian NYC (fancy tea room, w36th/9th)
[347 W 36th St] *fashion cafe with a plush decor for afternoon & high tea sets, meals set up like an English tea house with a French aesthetic w/croissants, pastries & desserts*

EATS

($)

The Halal Guys (famous Middle Eastern food cart at w53rd/6th)
[corner of W 53rd & 6th Ave] *NYC's famous Halal Guys food cart with a huge fanbase and long lines of fans & office regulars - chicken gyros, falafel platters & Middle Eastern rice plates*

El Sabroso (Ecuador/Peruvian food in building's loading dock, w37th/8th)
[265 W 37th S] *unique NY place & cheaper meal in area, popular chicken stew w/seating*

Empanada Mama - Hell's Kitchen (empanadas, 9th/w51st)
[765 9th Ave] *Latin focused food specializing in empanadas in narrow restaurant space w/seating, popular*

($$)

Capizzi (Italian brick oven pizza w/picture-perfect Neopolitan pizzas, 9th/w40th)
[547 9th Ave] *old-style Italian brick oven pizzeria w/charming decor, classic NY place*

Ippudo Westside (Japanese ramen, w51st/8th)
[321 W 51st St] *popular Japanese ramen shop chain in NYC, reliable place*

Hudson Yards (casual dining inside Hudson Yards mall complex, 34th/10th)
[20 Hudson Yards] *fast casual dining at Hudson Yards - Shake Shack, Mercado Little Spain eatery hall, Magnolia Bakery, Starbucks & Blue Bottle Coffee*

Mercato (well-regarded Italian restaurant, w39th/9th)
[352 W 39th St] *highly regarded and affordable Italian restaurant with warm & cozy interior, authentic Italian cuisines and pastas, Michelin-listed*

Sullivan St. Bakery (famous bakery & bread cafe, w47th/11th)
[533 W 47th St] *famous bakery cafe near High Line w/Bomboloni Italian donuts, breads, sandwiches, well known for breads & cookbooks, w/seating, highly regarded*

Sfilatino Italian Gourmet (Italian gourmet sandwiches, w57th/9th)
[342 W 57th St] *well regarded cafe focused on gourmet Italian sandwiches, coffee and rich desserts, wood counter and painted map interior w/seating & tables*

Pure Thai Cookhouse (neighborhood Thai restaurant, w51st/9th)
[766 9th Ave] *shophouse-style Thai restaurant in a rustic interior w/seating, serves homemade noodles & favorite Thai dishes, popular in neighborhood*

Friedman's Hell's Kitchen (American comfort food, breakfast, lunch, 10th/w35th)
[450 10th Ave] *popular brunch place & lunch spot with American comfort food*

Totto Ramen Hell's Kitchen (Japanese ramen, w51st/8th)
[464 W 51st St] *authentic Japanese ramen spot in theater district, highly rated & well regarded w/close quarter seating, usually has lines, popular*

Vintner Wine Market (wine & cheese shop w/eaterie, 9th/w47th)
[671 9th Ave] *wine, beer & cheese store w/seating area - sandwiches, salads & fondue*

($$$)

Sushi of Gari 46 (fancy sushi, w46th/9th)
[347 W 46th St] *Japanese sushi restaurant, known for omakase, well regarded, reservations*

Hudson Yards (fine dining restaurants inside HYds mall complex, 34th/10th)
[20 Hudson Yards] *work/play/food complex in Midtown West that is the new NYC attraction in fine dining often with city river views from the Hudson Yards complex including: The Tavern (American), Queensyard (Contemporary), Greywind (American), Peak (American), Estiatorio Milos (Mediterranean) Electric Lemon (American) or eat open-market style in Mercado Little Spain (Eataly-like Spanish food market)*

DRINKS & BARS

($)

Rudy's Bar & Grill (dive bar, 9th/w44th)
[627 9th Ave] *dive bar w/cheap beer, free hot dogs, jukebox & a pig mascot outside*

The Gaf West (laid back neighborhood pub, w48th/9th)
[401 W 48th St] *low key neighborhood bar with craft beer, generous happy hour specials every night, a few sports screens, comedy shows, dart boards & a jukebox.*

($$)

As Is NYC (craft beer, gastropub, 10th/w50th)
[328 W 45th St] *urban craft beer bar in a dimly lit, good-looking brick loft space w/roomy interior, gourmet quality food & large selection of craft beers*

Beer Culture (craft beer bar, w45th/8th)
[328 W 45th St] *laid back beer bar where you can choose your own beers from the fridges and pay at the bar, a well-kept cozy space*

Hellcat Annie's Tap Room (microbrewery craft beer on tap, 10th/w45th)
[637 10th Ave] *craft beer bar with woodsy inn decor and cask barrel tables, planked wood all around & beer boards to keep track of all the Porters & IPAs they have on tap, w/pub food*

Jasper's Taphouse +Kitchen (craft beer sports bar, 9th/w51st)
[761 9th Ave] *festive neighborhood sports bar with upscale bar food, craft beer, good place to hang out, watch game or have lunch, well ordered*

Landmark Tavern (old-time Irish tavern, 11th/w46th)
[626 11th Ave] *est. 1868, old-time Irish tavern with traditional Irish fare, one part bar, other part sit-down restaurant w/shepherds pie, bangers & mash, building is a city landmark*

Vintner Wine Market (wine & cheese shop w/eaterie, 9th/w47th)
[671 9th Ave] *wine, beer & cheese store w/seating area - sandwiches, salads & fondue*

($$$)

Dutch Fred's (cocktail bar, gastropub, w47th/8th)
[313 W 47th] *popular cocktail bar, speakeasy and gastropub with 1920's style decor, chicken waffles, named after the guy who coined the term "Hell's Kitchen"*

Hudson Yards (fine dining restaurants inside HYds mall complex, 34th/10th)
[20 Hudson Yards] *work/play/food complex in Midtown West that is the new NYC attraction in fine dining often with city river views from the Hudson Yards complex including: The Tavern (American), Queensyard (Contemporary), Greywind (American), Peak (American), Estiatorio Milos (Mediterranean) Electric Lemon (American) or eat open-market style in Mercado Little Spain (Eataly-like Spanish food market)*

SHOPPING

Hudson Yards (shopping/eats/entertainment complex, 34th/10th)
[20 Hudson Yards] *shopping and eating in Hudson Yards complex - Uniqlo, Muji, luxury stores, designer shops, eateries & boutiques*

The Drama Book Shop (bookstore w/plays, scripts & readings, w39th/8th)
[266 W 39th St] *bookstore with all things film, theater & TV, books from screenplays to musicals to in-store readings with ornate spiral book displays, a cafe inside & comfy couches to read in*

Shops at Columbus Circle (Time Warner Center, ColumbusCrcl/w59th)
[10 Columbus Circle] *mall complex in Time Warner Center at Columbus Circle featuring shops like Williams Sonoma cookware, H&M clothing, J.Crew clothing, TUMI luggage, Jo Malone London fragrances, Alo yoga activeware, Lululemon activewear, La Maison du Chocolat, Ladurée macarons, Moleskin stationary, luxury brand stores, fancy restaurants, Jazz at Lincoln Center & a Whole Foods on the basement level*

Vintner Wine Market (wine & cheese shop w/eaterie, 9th/w47th)
[671 9th Ave] *wine, beer & cheese store w/seating area - sandwiches, salads & fondue*

FUN STUFF

Escape Room NYC - Mission Escape Games (escape room game room,w 37th/8th)
[265 W 37th St Suite 802A] *escape rooms are movie set-style rooms that groups of people book for an hour solve the puzzles inside together to escape it, can book different rooms online (other Escape Rooms Game Challenges are in this area too)*

AMC 34th Street 14 Movie Theater (movie theater, w34th/8th)
[312 W 34th St] *the big movie theater multiplex in the area, w/IMAX theater*

MANHATTAN VIEWS & ATTRACTIONS

Hudson Yards (shopping / food /entertainment center, 34thst/10th)
[20 Hudson Yards] *work/play/food complex in Midtown West that is the new NYC attraction with shopping (Uniqlo, Muji, luxury stores, designer shops & boutiques) eating (Shake Shack , Little Spain, fine dining) and visitor attractions within the Hudson Yards complex - The Edge, a sky deck observatory and The Vessel, a walkable building sculpture with views (upper floors closed to the public), it is also the entry/exit point of the popular High Line city-walk park in midtown*

The Edge (suspended glass sky deck observatory w/NYC views, @ Hudson Yards)
[Hudson Yards] *contemporary-designed, sleek triangular sky deck observatory that's suspended over 100 stories high with see-through glass floor, angled glass walls and 360-degree spectacular views of NYC to give the feeling of floating above the city, can reserve tickets online, @$36-$54 tkts*

The Vessel (walk-up building structure/attraction @Hudson Yards)
centerpiece attraction at Hudson Yards, building sculpture you can climb to see views
Note: *The Vessel's upper floors are closed to the public, only base floor & plaza area are open*

The High Line (elevated park walk on former train tracks to Chelsea, @34th St Hudson Yards entrance) [no restrooms on High line, only at Hudson Yds or Chelsea Mkt]
[20 Hudson Yards] *a top NYC attraction, formerly abandoned, elevated railroad track converted into a modern park and walking path area 22 blocks long from Chelsea Market to Hudson Yards with unique, immersive city views*

Intrepid Sea, Air & Space Museum (Pier 86, 12th/w46th)
[Pier 86, W 46th St] *military and space museum at Pier 86 where you can explore the retired Intrepid Aircraft carrier, see the first Space Shuttle, submarines and airplanes close up, docked along the Hudson River on the West side at Pier 86*

Javits Convention Center (big shows, fairs & events center, 34th/11th)
[429 11th Ave] *major convention center of NYC for auto shows, comic cons, big fairs and events, large complex that is now connected to 34th St/Hudson Yds stop on 7 train, order events tickets at Javitz Center online*

MIDTOWN
34th St, Garment District, Macy's

quick directions
Take 1, 2, 3 downtown to 34th St - Penn Station stop [w34th/7thAve]

COFFEE

Stumptown Coffee Roasters (coffee shop in front of Ace Hotel, w29th/Broadway)
[18 W 29th St] *popular coffee shop serving Stumptown coffee with standing window tables, can also bring your drinks into the dimly lit lounge area of Ace Hotel via the connected lobby w/comfortable couches, lounge chairs, tables & Wifi in stylish surroundings*

Culture Espresso (stylish coffee shop w/award winning choc chip cookie, w38th/6th)
[72 W 38th St] *tasteful cozy cafe with a chic décor, serves coffee, baked items including its award-winning chocolate chip cookie, w/seating, Wifi (no bathroom)*

King's Street Coffee (good-sized neighborhood coffee shop, w30th/6th)
[121 W 30th St] *good-sized neighborhood cafe in tidy, spartan interior space that serve's Joe's Coffee, matcha lattes, Balthazar pastries w/seating, Wifi*

Old Country Coffee (cafe near High Line, w34th/9th)
[455 W 34th St] *quirky & earthy rustic cafe near the High Line, coffee and pastries in a fun country-cabin interior w/plenty of seating & tables, Wifi*

Bluestone Lane Garment District Coffee Shop (coffee shop, Broadway/37th)
[1375 Broadway] *Aussie-inspired coffee chain with food and pastries, big on avocado toast w/upstairs seating area (no Wifi)*

TEA

Grace Street Coffee & Desserts (popular tea & dessert place in Koreatown, w32nd/Broadway)
[17 W 32nd St] *roomy & popular dessert place in Koreatown serving matcha lattes and milk teas along with sumptuous inventive desserts - Basque Burnt Cheesecake, Matcha Beignets w/green tea ice cream & giant shaved snow sundaes*

Machi Machi (bubble tea shop in Koreatown, w32nd/Broadway)
[33 W 32nd St] *bubble tea shop in Koreatown with bubble teas, milk teas, cream cheese foam teas & tea lattes in a food stand space*

TeaMakers (tea stand in Koreatown, w32nd/Broadway)
[15 W 32nd St] *tea stand in Koreatown serving milk teas, fruit teas and cheese foam teas near the Empire State Building*

EATS

($)

Krispy Kreme (donut shop, near Macy's, 6th/w37th)
[994 6th Ave] *est. 1937, beloved art deco era donut chain, famous for its glazed donuts baked on premises, returns to NYC w/10 ct boxes of donut holes, more grab & go, often has lines*

Woorjip Authentic Korean Food (Korean buffet, w32nd/5th)
[12 W 32nd St] *tasty Korean hot food buffet in Koreatown w/prepared foods, hot food bar, inexpensive w/seating, takeout & groceries*

Kati Roll Company (Indian roti rolls, fast food place, w39th/6th)
[49 W 39th St] *Indian roti rolls, quality meat & veggies in build-you-own format chicken tikka roll, flat breads w/seating*

($$)

Andrews NYC Diner (reliable old school NY diner w/booths, 7th/w35th)
[463 7th Ave] *no-frills, family owned NYC diner that's centrally located in area near Penn Station and Macy's w/classic diner interior and comfortable booth seating, good food for breakfast, lunch, dinner, always busy, bustling, reliable & well regarded*

Black Iron Burger (burger place, w38th/7th)
[245 W 38th St] *well made specialty burgers with craft beers, considered a top NYC cheeseburger, easygoing and cozy atmosphere in rustic-brick setting, popular*

Ichiran Ramen (classic & famous tonkotso ramen place in NYC since 1960, w31st/7th)
[132 W 31st St] *old-time ramen chain that's famous in New York & Japan, has been serving tonkotso ramen (pork-bone based soup ramen) in classic tradition, in NYC since 1960 at this spot, w/seating at tables & single booths w/no tipping, food destination for ramen lovers*

Tonchin NY Ramen (popular Tokyo ramen chain, tonkutsu ramen, w36th/5thAve)
[13 W 36th St] *NYC branch of popular ramen chain from Tokyo that specializes in tonkotso ramen & grilled dishes, Michelin ranked, on fancier side w/seating*

Shake Shack Herald Square (burger place near Macy's, Broadway/w36th)
[1333 Broadway] *popular NYC burger chain, often on best burger lists, near Macy's w/seating & standing tables, often crowded, can grab & go or use patio tables on street plazas*

Friedman's Herald Square (American comfort food near Herald Sq, 31st/6th)
[132 W 31st St] *popular place for American comfort food, burgers, locally sourced ingredients, warm rustic interior w/seating*

Mercato (well-regarded Italian restaurant, w39th/9th)
[352 W 39th St] *highly regarded and affordable Italian restaurant with warm & cozy interior, authentic Italian cuisines and pastas, Michelin-listed*

The Picnic Basket (gourmet sandwiches, w37th/6th)
[65 W 37th St] *small shop with gourmet quality sandwiches & paninis, breakfast sandwiches w/limited seating, popular in the area, can have lines at lunchtime, more grab & go*

Alidoro - Bryant Park (Italian sandwich shop, e39th/Madison)
[18 E 39th St] *authentic Italian gourmet sandwiches in fancy midtown branch of the highly regarded Soho sandwich shop w/seating in a lofty stylish interior*

Luke's Lobster Garment District (lobster roll, seafood, Broadway/w39th)
[1407 Broadway] *Maine Lobster rolls, crab, seafood in seafood shack space w/limited seating*

Beyond Sushi (veggie sushi, w37th/7th)
[134 W 37th St] *creative vegetarian sushi rolls, vegan dumplings, noodle bowls, spacious w/seating*

Koreatown
Many good restaurants and places by 32nd St & Broadway:

Jongro BBQ (Korean bbq, 2nd Fl, w32nd/Broadway)
[22 W 32nd] *big Korean barbecue joint, atmospheric, energetic & lively, lots of seating*

Barn Joo 35 (Korean fusion, w35th/6th)
[34 W 35th St] *trendy Korean fusion, Korean tapas, has bar with music*

Woorjip Authentic Korean Food (Korean buffet, w32nd/5th)
[12 W 32nd St] *tasty Korean hot food buffet in Koreatown w/prepared foods, hot food bar, inexpensive w/seating, takeout & groceries*

Tous Les Jours Bakery + Cafe (Korean French bakery, w32nd/Broadway)
[31 W 32nd St] *spacious Korean French bakery, serves coffee, pastry & cakes w/seating*

Grace Street Coffee & Desserts (popular tea & dessert place in Koreatown, w32nd/Broadway)
[17 W 32nd St] *roomy & popular dessert place in Koreatown serving matcha lattes and milk teas along with sumptuous inventive desserts - Basque Burnt Cheesecake, Matcha Beignets w/green tea ice cream & giant shaved snow sundaes*

DRINKS & BARS

($)

Blue Ruin (rock & roll dive bar, 9th/40th)
[538 9th Ave] *dive bar with hard rock edge, jukebox, loud music & cheap beer*

($$)

Reichenbach Hall (German beer hall & eats, like Octoberfest in NYC, w37th/5th)
[5 W 37th St] *festive German beer hall with long wood benches and high ceilings in a warm architectural hall interior serving beer steins, schnitzels, sausages, bratwurst, sauerkraut, warm pretzels & German specialties, Octoberfest-style place*

Slattery's Midtown Pub (classic Irish NYC pub near Empire State Bldg, e36th/5th)
[8 E 36th St] *classic double-decker NYC Irish pub in midtown with a cozy, darkly wooded interior & patio over street, serving pub food with happy hour specials*

District Tap House (craft beer, gastropub, w38th/8th)
[246 W 38th St] *large beer selection & gourmet food in big tavern space, w/seating & booths*

($$$)

Refinery Rooftop (rooftop bar on top of Refinery Hotel, w38th/6th)
[63 W 38th St] *rooftop bar in warm and relaxed environment, a spacious lounge of exposed brick and wood, comfortable chairs, couches, tables, fireplaces all around, retractable glass roof & outside patio w/immersive city views of Empire State Bldg, pricey*

Monarch Rooftop (rooftop bar by Herald Sq, w35th/6th)
[71 W 35th St] *rooftop bar atop Courtyard Marriott hotel serving cocktails and drinks with Empire State and Herald Sq views, in a comfortable lounge bar interior & outside space*

The Skylark (rooftop bar & interior lounge, 30 stories up, w39th/7th)
[200 W 39th St] *rooftop bar that's more of an interior wrap around lounge with couches, seating and window views from 30th floor, gets dimly lit with night views of city, Midtown & Empire State Building, opens rooftop patio area in the nicer weather months, pricey*

SHOPPING

Macy's (NYC 's most famous & biggest department store, w34th/Broadway)
[151 W 34th St] *NYC institution since 1858, Macy's is the largest and most famous department store in the city, a classic all-purpose store that covers everybody and sells nearly everything from clothes to furniture, even has old-time wooden escalators on some floors, generally affordable and always running weekly sales*

Sample Sales in Garment District
[Garment District] *Many sample sales take place in the Garment District. Sample sales are usually high-end brands and designer merchandise that sell their overstock at marked down prices at a pop up store address for a week or so. Those in the know shop this way to get better sales and cheaper deals on nicer stuff, especially from the high end brands. Blogs, social media & Instagrams are good ways to keep track of the best sample sales in the city — from clothes, jackets, handbags, hats, backpacks to stationary supplies, kitchen & house items*

B&H Photo (photo & video superstore w/good reputation, 9th/w34th)
[420 9th Ave] *largest photography and video equipment store in city, known for covering all things photos and electronics in NY, a big operation with intricate conveyor belt setup, specialty areas and showrooms throughout this massive store space, has good reputation*

Shopping around 34th St (on 34th St, btw 5th & 8th Ave, near Macy's)
[34th St] *brand stores and shopping on 34th St and around Macy's area*

OUTDOOR PUBLIC SPACES

Herald Square (city park & outdoor plaza, w34th/Broadway)
[W 34th St & Broadway] *small triangular park near Macy's that's a good place to relax in a busy area, next to street plazas w/patio seating, public restrooms & coffee*

FUN STUFF

AMC 34th Street 14 (movie theater, w34th/8th)
[312 W 34th St] *big movie theater multiplex in the area, w/IMAX theater*

ATTRACTIONS & MANHATTAN VIEWS

Empire State Building (iconic art deco skyscraper in NYC skyline, w34/5th)
[350 Fifth Ave] *famous & iconic 1930s art deco skyscraper of the NYC skyline that's a major tourist attraction for its stunning views, usually crowded w/long waits, @$44-$79 tkts*

The Morgan Library & Museum (art museum w/focus on drawings & the graphic arts, w/concert hall & cafe (Madison/e37th)
[225 Madison Ave] *art museum & architectural landmark that used to be the private library of J.P. Morgan, known for its focus on master drawings and graphic arts exhibitions, w/lavish private library room, concerts, events, museum cafe, can reserve free tickets online in advance for Fri nights from 5-7 pm*

CHELSEA
The High Line, Chelsea Market

quick directions
Take A, C, E, L downtown to 14th St / 8th Ave stop [w14th/8thAve]

COFFEE

Intelligentsia Coffee Highline Coffeebar (coffee bar in lobby of High Line Hotel, 10th/w20th)
[180 10th Ave] *cafe espresso bar in lobby of High Line Hotel, serving Intelligentsia coffee w/seating in lobby & outdoor patio space, Wifi*

Variety Coffee Roasters (coffee shop w/big space to study, 7th/w25th)
[261 7th Ave] *classic deco-looking coffee shop, arched wood ceiling, fancy tiled floor, lots of space w/seating for studying & relaxing in mid-century ambience, Wifi*

Yanni's Coffee (neighborhood coffee shop, 7thave/w16th)
[96 7th Ave] *mid-sized neighborhood coffee shop in a well put-together, large windowed space, homemade choc chip cookie w/some seating, well regarded, Wifi*

Old Country Coffee (cafe near High Line, w34th/9th)
[455 W 34th St] *quirky & earthy rustic cafe near the High Line, coffee and pastries in fun country cabin interior w/plenty of seating & tables, Wifi*

Bluestone Lane Chelsea Piers Cafe (Chelsea Piers, Pier 62, 11th /w22nd)
[62 Chelsea Piers] *Aussie-inspired coffee chain, pastries and food, big on avocado toast, in large two-level space with wide patio seating in front w/Manhattan views (no Wifi)*

La Colombe Coffee Roasters (coffee shop, w27th/11th)
[601 W 27th St] *upscale stylish coffee chain in a lofty, modern wood space w/good seating in 27th St Terminal Warehouse industrial space (no Wifi)*

Starbucks Reserve Roastery (Starbucks deluxe roastery, 9th Ave/w15th)
[61 9th Ave] *Willy Wonka factory-looking Starbucks w/pipes & machines all around, showcasing new concepts in a big multi-level space, lots of seating, Wifi*

TEA

Matchaful Cafe (matcha cafe stand inside Whole Foods, w33rd/10th)
[450 W 33rd St] *matcha latte cafe & vegan matcha soft serve stand inside Whole Foods, also serves chai lattes, teas, pastries and desserts*

Tea & Sympathy (tea room & British restaurant, Greenwich/Jane)
[108 Greenwich Ave] *British tea room with inn decor that celebrates all things British, serves afternoon tea & crumpets, English comfort food w/table seating*

EATS

($)

Dil-e Punjab Deli (Indian deli & eatery, 9th/w31st)
[170 9th Ave] *authentic Indian food plate at deli, cheap & plentiful meal that's popular with cabbies and locals, limited seating, grab & go*

Johny's Luncheonette (old school luncheonette serving all-day breakfast, w25th/6th)
[124 W 25th St] *small counter diner luncheonette serving all-day breakfast & reasonably priced lunch specials at a steady pace*

($$)

Pisillo Italian Panini Chelsea (authentic Italian panini sandwiches, w25th/6th)
[124 W 25th St] small shop serving grilled or toasted Italian panini sandwiches

Chelsea Market (food hall/market, can enter from the High Line, 9th/w15th)
[75 9th Ave] *downtown food hall and tourist destination, both a working market and foodie wonderland, assortment of eateries and shops in industrial bricked, artsy hall space - The Lobster Place, Los Tacos No.1, Friedman's Lunch, Creamline American classics, Doughnuttery, - can also enter/exit the High Line elevated park walk here*

The Grey Dog - Chelsea (cafe/restaurant, American comfort food, w16th/8th)
[242 W 16th St] *cozy, rustic place with American comfort food, better for breakfast or lunch, w/seating, Wifi, popular*

Sullivan St. Bakery (bakery cafe near High Line, 9th/w24th)
[236 9th Ave] *famous bakery cafe, bomboloni (Italian donuts), sandwiches, breads, well known for breads & cookbooks, w/seating, highly regarded*

Fonda (small & cozy Mexican gourmet restaurant, 9th/21st)
[189 9th Ave] *intimate Mexican restaurant near the High Line, a neighbor favorite that specializes in enchiladas, guacamole & authentic Mexican cuisine*

($$$)

The Cookshop (upscale American comfort food, near High Line, 10th/w19th)
[156 10th Ave] *upscale casual restaurant serving farm-to-table and American comfort food with a reputation for culinary excellence & consistency, very popular*

Cull & Pistol Oyster Bar (in Chelsea Mkt, seafood & oyster bar, 9h/w15th)
[75 9th Ave] *intimate raw bar & oyster bar in Chelsea Mkt, happy hours w/oysters special*

The Mermaid Inn Chelsea (casual seafood restaurant/oyster bar, 10th/w23rd)
[227 10th Ave] *casual, classy seafood restaurant in nautically decorated restaurant space focused on sustainably sourced, happy hours specials with mixed drinks & seafood appetizers*

($$$$)

Sushi Seki Chelsea (fancy sushi, w23rd/7th)
[208 W 23rd St] *well regarded Japanese sushi restaurant, chef omakase, Michelin rated, expensive, reservations*

DRINKS & BARS

($$)

Porchlight (atmospheric cocktail bar, 11th/w28th)
[271 11th Ave] *cocktail bar in large industrial space with Southern twist, roomy w/ seating, furniture & ambiance, service included in price*

Barcade (bar w/arcade games, w24th/7th)
[148 W 24th St] *spacious bar with arcade games and craft beer, retro 80's/90's video game arcades*

Crompton Ale House (upscale Irish pub near Mad Sq Garden, w26th/7th)
[159 W 26th St] *upscale tavern w/book-lined shelves and warm dark-wood interior, favorite of after work crowd w/sports TVs, craft beer, happy hours & comfort food*

The Tippler (subterranean cozy cocktail & craft beer bar under Chelsea Mkt, w15th/9th)
[425 W 15th St] *cocktail & craft beer bar in reclaimed wood & brick space under Chelsea Mkt w/antique fixtures, Persian rugs and vintage décor to relax in*

SHOPPING

Chelsea Market (food hall/market, can enter from the High Line, 9th/w15th)
[75 9th Ave] *downtown food hall and tourist destination, both a working market and foodie wonderland, assortment of eateries and shops in industrial bricked, artsy hall space - The Lobster Place, Los Tacos No.1, Friedman's Lunch, Creamline American classics, Doughnuttery, - can also enter/exit the High Line elevated park walk here*

Muji Chelsea (Japanese items, clothes, w19th/5th)
[16 W 19th St] *Japanese office and art supplies, house items, clothing store with tasteful and elegant products, more low-key downtown branch of Muji that's easy to browse*

Housing Works Thrift Shop - Chelsea (thrift store, w17th/6th)
[143 W 17th St] *good chain of NY thrift stores that are well ordered and pleasant to shop at, tend to sell affordable high end used clothes and stuff that reflects the neighborhood, has charitable mission behind it*

Stores and shops around Chelsea area
[Chelsea] *stores scattered around side streets & main avenues, centralized on 23rd st, 6th Ave*

MANHATTAN VIEWS & OUTDOOR PUBLIC SPACES

The High Line (elevated park walk on former train tracks to Chelsea, @14h St /10th Ave Chelsea entrance) [no restrooms on High line, only at Hudson Yds or Chelsea Mkt] [20 Hudson Yards] *a top NYC attraction, formerly abandoned, elevated railroad track converted into a modern park and walking path area 22 blocks long from Chelsea Market to Hudson Yards with unique, immersive city views*

Hudson River Park (park by Hudson, WestSt/w10th up to w59th St) [West St] *scenic river walk on Hudson River with biking and walking lanes, parks w/waterfront views, picnic areas & places to relax*

Little Island (man-made, fantasy island park on the water at Pier 55) [Pier 55 @ Hudson River Park, 14th St by Chelsea Mkt] *Man-made, architecturally created island that was converted from a damaged pier from Hurricane Sandy into a park/fantasy island off the Chelsea Piers that serves as a public space and recreational park*

FUN STUFF & ATTRACTIONS

Chelsea Market (food hall/market, can enter from the High Line, 9th/w15th) [75 9th Ave] *downtown food hall and tourist destination, both a working market and foodie wonderland, assortment of eateries and shops in industrial bricked, artsy hall space - The Lobster Place, Los Tacos No.1, Friedman's Lunch, Creamline American classics, Doughnuttery, - can also enter/exit the High Line elevated park walk here*

Whitney Museum of American Art (Amer. art museum, Gansevoort/w10th) [99 Gansevoort St] *new home of Whitney Art museum that came over from Upper East Side, American art from past to present, pay what-you-wish on Fridays 7-10pm*

Chelsea Art Galleries (mostly on 18th-27th St, btw 10th & 11th) [btw 10 & 11th Ave] *Chelsea is the contemporary gallery center of NYC from 18th to 27th streets are major contemporary art galleries w/art shows and exhibitions*

Chelsea Piers (sports & entertainment complex atHudson River Park, 11th/w21st) [62 Chelsea Piers] *huge waterfront sports & entertainment complex - between 17th and 23rd St on Hudson River with a golf club w/multi-story driving range, a field house with a fitness health club, ice rinks, bowling alley, several events w/dining and shopping*

FLATIRON DISTRICT
Downtown & 23rd St

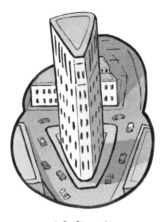

quick directions
Take N, Q, R,W downtown to 23 St stop [e23rd/5thAve]

COFFEE

Devoción (popular & stylish coffeeshop, e20th/Broadway)
[25 E 20th St] *inviting coffee shop in a long brick-wood loft space with a cozy aesthetic, Columbia farm-to-table coffee, espressos, nitro brews & pastries w/seating, couches, Wifi (no Wifi on weekends)*

Paper Coffee (coffee bar in Made Hotel lobby, w29th/6th)
[44 W 29th St] *coffee bar in swank Made Hotel lobby, chic wood interior and stylish modern ski lodge look to it all, food, pastries, roomy w/relaxing seating & tables, Wifi*

Gotham Coffee Roasters (coffee shop, w19th/5th)
[23 W 19th St] *small coffee shop in a well put together, boxy interior behind a full pane window, espressos, pour-overs, pastries & some seating (no Wifi, no bathroom)*

Ralph's Coffee (relaxing sidewalk coffee spot on 5th Ave by Ralph Lauren, 5th/w21st)
[160 5th Ave] *fashionable coffee place in downtown 5th Ave with a fun, classic retro decor serving coffee, lattes & tea with pastries, desserts with a nice sidewalk space to hang out at, Wifi (no bathroom)*

TEA

Jin Yun Fu Tea Shop (Chinese tea house & shop, w25th/Madison)
[40 W 25th St Fl 2, Ste 224] *Chinese tea house with elegant decor and tea rooms that focuses on art of tea with tea sessions, reservations for sessions, check for walk-in times*

Teazzi Tea Shop (bubble tea shop, w14th/6th)
[47 W 14th St] *well regarded bubble tea spot with selection of fancy bubble teas, milk teas, hot teas, fruit teas, oolong teas, honey golden & taro lattes*

Patisserie Chanson (fancy dessert pastry shop w/afternoon high tea, w23rd/5th)
[20 W 23rd St] *fancy French pastry dessert shop near Flatiron, has afternoon tea set service w/sandwiches, cakes, macarons & pastries*

EATS

($)

Pret A Manger (prepared food, organic & coffee, 6th/w20th)
[655 6th Ave] *sandwiches, soups, salads, coffee, pastry, reliable place with seating, booths, Wifi*

Dough Doughnuts (handmade artisanal donuts, w19th/5th)
[14 W 19th St] *handmade artisanal donut cafe in loft space where they bake the donuts in the back, w/seating*

($$)

Shake Shack Madison Square Park (burgers, great location to dine outside at the original Shake Shack in MadSqPark, Madison/e23rd,)
[E 23rd St, Madison Square Park] *best location of beloved NYC burger chain that is always on top burger lists, Shake Shack started here in Madison Square Park outside on these beautiful park grounds w/plentiful patio seating, fun dining experience in the park*

Eataly NYC Flatiron (Italian food hall across from Madison Sq Pk, 5th/w23rd)
[200 5th Ave] *Italian gourmet food hall that's a big foodie destination w/breads, cheeses, seafoods, meats, pizza, pastas, markets and beer garden on roof, large space w/seating in areas*

Maman Nomad (gourmet French American cafe & bakery, w25th/5th)
[22 W 25th St] *stylish French American cafe with elegant gourmet aesthetic, sandwiches, breakfast, brunch, coffee, bakery w/wood table seating, Wifi*

Ootoya Chelsea (Japanese comfort food, w18th/5th)
[8 W 18th St] *chain from Japan with authentic Japanese comfort food, pork cutlet, chirashi bowl, roomy with a no-tipping custom, popular*

Tacombi (popular, festive Mexican tacquerias in NYC, w24th/6th)
[30 W 24th St] *Mexican neighborhood-style taqueria chain with tacos, burritos, enchiladas, juice bar & margaritas w/table seating in large Mexico canteen-like setting*

Dig (farm fresh marketbowl, e23rd/Madison)
[16 E 23rd St] *fast casual food chain w/farm fresh marketbowl in big-sized cafeteria space w/plenty of seating, reliable*

DRINKS & BARS

($$)

Broken Shaker at Freehand NY (rooftop bar on top of Freehand Hotel, Lex/w24th)
[23 Lexington Ave] *outdoor/indoor style rooftop bar on top of Freehand Hotel w/ garden nooks and patio space & indoor wicker chairs and lanterns, w/views of Flatiron & Midtown*

Turnmill Bar (popular craft beer & cocktail bar in Flatiron, e27th/Park)
[119 E 27th St] *stylish rustic craft beer and cocktail bar w/wood-planked interior, fireplace & candle lighting, limited food options, happy hours, can get crowded*

Barcade (bar w/arcade games, w24th/7th)
[148 W 24th St] *spacious bar with arcade games and craft beer, retro 80's/90's video game arcades*

($$$)

Flatiron Room (rooftop bar, 5th/w27th)
[230 5th Ave] *plush, spacious interior space, dimly lit for fine dining, cocktails, known for over 1000 whiskey varieties & live jazz shows in their curtain lounge area*

230 Fifth Rooftop Lounge (rooftop bar, 5th/w27th)
[230 5th Ave] *rooftop bar with splendid views of NYC and Empire State Building, roomy and spacious w/seating, a social destination that gets big crowds, pricey*

SERRA by Birreria at Eataly (beer garden on top of Eataly, 5th/w23rd)
[200 5th Ave] *mid-sized garden atrium decorated with flowers on top of Eataly with popular bar & dining tables for Eataly's offerings, more for ambience, no views really, pricey*

SHOPPING

Rizzoli Bookstore (art & design bookstore, Broadway/w23rd)
[1133 Broadway] *stylish prestige bookstore in heart of Flatiron district known for art, photography, fashion and design books and its elegant and refined presentation, well-curated in modern space with spacious event area*

Housing Works Thrift Shop Gramercy (thrift store, e23rd/3rd Ave)
[157 E 23rd St] *good chain of NY thrift stores that are well ordered and pleasant to shop at, tends to sell affordable high end used clothes and stuff that reflects the neighborhood, has charitable mission behind it*

Muji Chelsea (Japanese items, clothes, w19th/5th)
[16 W 19th St] *Japanese office and art supplies, house items, clothing store with tasteful and elegant products, more low-key downtown branch of Muji that's easy to browse*

Bottlerocket Wine & Spirit (neighborhood wine shop, w19th/5th)
[5 W 19th St] *award-winning, well-ordered wine shop, organizes wine by themes*

Fishs Eddy (kitchen/cookware, Broadway/w19th)
[889 Broadway] *affordable kitchenware, stocked with bargain baskets full of practical, retro and kitschy cookware & cupware priced to sell*

Downtown shopping on 5th Ave & 6th Ave (btw 14th St & 23rd St)
[5th Ave/6th Ave] *downtown stores for clothing, designer brands, boutiques and other shops on 5th Ave, 6th Ave and parts of Broadway, also on 23rd St*

OUTDOOR PUBLIC SPACES

Madison Square Park (elegant city park, Madison/e23rd)
[Madison Ave at E 23rd St] *gorgeous French-styled park at 23rd & Madison, elegant and pleasant to stroll in, restored from neglect into a wonderful park with great views and water fountains, can dine at the original Shake Shack which started here on its park grounds*

Flatiron Plaza (city plaza around Flatiron building & Mad Sq Park, 5th/w23rd)
[175 5th Ave] *many outside sidewalk tables and chairs with food stands around the Flatiron Building, Madison Sq Park and Eataly, with great views of the Flatiron and downtown activity as you people-watch and relax, also can grab something at Shake Shack or Eataly to eat & sit outside in the plaza*

FLATIRON

ATTRACTIONS

Flatiron Building (famous building of downtown NYC w/city plaza, 5th/w23rd)
[175 5th Ave] *iconic, triangular ironworks 19th century building, city landmark of downtown NYC w/street plazas, can only look at from the outside but defines the area*

Madison Square Park (elegant city park, Madison/e23rd)
[Madison Ave at 23rd st] *gorgeous French-styled park at 23rd & Madison, elegant and pleasant to stroll in, restored from neglect into a wonderful park with great views and water fountains, can dine at the original Shake Shack which started here on its park grounds*

Eataly NYC Flatiron (Italian food hall across from Madison Sq Pk, 5th/w23rd)
[200 5th Ave] *Italian gourmet food hall that's a big foodie destination w/breads, cheeses, seafoods, meats, pizza, pastas, markets and beer garden on roof, large space w/seating in areas*

UNION SQUARE
Downtown & 14th St

quick directions
Take 1, 2, 3, 4, 5, 6, N, R,W downtown to Union Sq stop [14th/UnionSqW]

COFFEE

Everyman Espresso (coffee shop, cappuccinos, next to a dance school, e13th/3rd)
[136 E 13th St] *artsy 80's era coffee shop known for its cappuccinos & espressos with good amount of seating and tables, next to a dance school, Wifi*

Joe Coffee (coffee shop, e13th/5th)
[9 E 13th St] *mid-sized cafe from NY chain of coffee shops, coffee & pastries, reliable place w/seating (no Wifi)*

O Cafe (neighborhood corner cafe, 6th/w12th)
[482 6th Ave] *solid corner coffee shop with Brazilian coffee & pastries (such as Brazilian cheese bread), well-ordered wood interior, organic & locally sourced food, looks like it could be a cafe in Sweden with New York views, good hangout place w/seating (no Wifi)*

Irving Farm New York Coffee Roasters (roomy cafe, e18th/Irving Place)
[71 Irving Pl] *original store of Irving Farm coffee chain in good-sized rustic space, coffee, food, pastries, roomy w/seating, tables, gets crowded (no Wifi)*

Daily Provisions Union Square (roomy cafe, e19th/Park)
[103 E 19th St] *good-sized cafe & bakery by restaurateur who started Shake Shack, gourmet coffee, pastries, cookies, breakfast & comfort foods w/sidewalk seating, Wifi*

Blue Bottle Coffee (coffee shop, UniversityPl/e12th)
[101 University Place] *SF coffee roaster chain, pour over coffee, limited seating, more grab & go (no Wifi)*

TEA

Lady Mendl's Tea Salon (fancy tea room in Gramercy Park, Irving Pl/e17th)
[56 Irving Pl] *English style tea salon in Gramercy Park, old world-styled Victorian interior setting w/couches, lounge chairs & hardwood floors, prix-fixe specials, pricey*

Teazzi Tea Shop (bubble tea shop, w14th/6th)
[47 W 14th St] *well-regarded bubble tea spot with selection of fancy bubble teas, milk teas, hot teas, fruit teas, oolong teas, honey golden & taro lattes*

EATS

($)

Joe Jr. Diner (classic NYC diner, comfort food, w18th/5th)
[167 3rd Ave] *classic NYC diner that's a staple in the neighborhood, w/booths & bar stool seating serving affordable diner fare - burger, fries, pastrami sandwiches, egg sandwiches, pancakes, breakfast*

Pret A Manger (prepared food, organic & coffee, Broadway/e17th)
[857 Broadway] *reliable corner spot in heart of Union Square w/sandwiches, soups, salads, coffee, pastry, also upstairs seating area that has roomy booths & Wifi*

Union Square Market (largest NYC greenmarket in plaza, 14th/Broadway)
[Union Sq Plaza] *the largest NYC greenmarket at Union Sq Plaza - M, W, F & Sat, farm fresh produce and eats with benches, patio seating & tables in middle park area*

Whole Foods Market Union Sq (dining area upstairs, UnionSqS/Broadway)
[4 Union Square South] *centrally located Whole Foods with hot food stations, salad bar, prepared foods w/dining area upstairs overlooking Union Sq. Plaza*

($$)

Ootoya Chelsea (Japanese restaurant, comfort food, w18th/5th)
[8 W 18th St] *chain from Japan with authentic Japanese comfort food, pork cutlet, chirashi bowl, roomy, no tipping custom, popular*

The Grey Dog Union Sq (cafe/restaurant, Amer. comfort food, UnivPl/e12th)
[90 University Pl] *cozy rustic place with American comfort food, better for breakfast or lunch w/seating, Wifi, popular*

Dough Doughnuts (handmade artisanal donuts, w19th/5th)
[14 W 19th St] *handmade artisanal donut cafe in loft space where they bake the donuts in the back w/seating*

DRINKS & BARS

($$)

Old Town Bar (old time NYC tavern, e18th/Broadway)
[45 E 18th St] *est. 1892, old time bar behind Union Sq, more for drinks in old NYC tavern ambience in a dark city saloon interior from yesteryear*

Lillie's Victorian Establishment (grand old bar with 19th century decor, e17th/Broadway)
[13 E 17th St] *fancy antique bar that could be from a time capsule with high ceilings and 19th century interior in a grand decorated space with restaurant inside serving traditional British fare with happy hour specials*

($$$)

The Raines Law Room Chelsea (fancy cocktail lounge, w17th/6th)
[48 W 17th St] *speakeasy fancy cocktail lounge, posh and dimly lit with old world elegance, separate rooms with different decor, pricey*

SHOPPING

Union Square Market (largest NYC greenmarket in plaza, 14th/Broadway)
[Union Sq Plaza] *the largest NYC greenmarket at Union Sq Plaza, market is every
M, W, F & Sat (8am-6pm) - farm fresh produce, eats w/benches & tables in middle park area*

Barnes & Noble bookstore (biggest bookstore in NYC w/large Starbucks cafe on
4th fl, 17th/Broadway)
[33 E 17th St] *mega-sized Barnes & Noble in Union Sq that is NYC's biggest bookstore
w/large Starbucks cafe on 4th floor, events and signings on top floor, good place for
browsing, relaxing or a meeting up downtown*

The Strand Bookstore (famous large used bookstore in NYC, Broadway/e12th)
[828 Broadway] *beloved used bookstore in a huge space w/three levels of rare books,
art books & used books, $1 book sales on sidewalk, iconic destination for book lovers*

Paragon Sports (big sporting goods shop near Union Sq, Broadway/18th)
[867 Broadway] *big sporting goods store of NYC near Union Sq, go-to place for all
things sports in the city, multi-level floors w/sports equipment, clothes, accessories*

Forbidden Planet (comic book, fantasy & hobby store, Broadway/w13th)
[832 Broadway] *big comics shop of downtown near Union Square & NYU with a
large selection of comics, graphic novels, games, toys & collectibles*

Books of Wonder (famous children's bookstore w/story time, w17th/6th)
[42 W 17th St] *independent destination bookstore for children's books readers big &
small w/author talks, story time readings, rare 1st editions & original book illustrations*

Academy Records & CDs (classic vintage record shop, w18th/5th)
[12 W 18th St] *old school used record store in NYC, selling vintage vinyl LPs & CDs at
bargain prices, more focused on classical & jazz than other genres, sells DVD movies & Blu-rays*

Beacon's Closet (thrift store, w13th/5thave)
[10 W 13th St] *one of major NYC thrift stores chains that buys, sells & trades used clothes,
good-sized city outpost of the bigger Brooklyn location, has wide range of used clothes -
everyday & eclectic designer clothes that reflect the area*

Fishs Eddy (kitchen/cookware, Broadway/w19th)
[889 Broadway] *affordable kitchenware, stocked with bargain baskets full of
practical, retro and kitschy cookware & cupware that are priced to sell*

OUTDOOR PUBLIC SPACES

Union Square (outdoor public plaza w/largest NYC greenmarket, 14th/Broadway)
[Union Sq Plaza] *the largest NYC greenmarket at Union Sq Plaza - M, W, F & Sat, (8am-6pm) farm fresh produce & eats w/benches, patio seating & tables in middle park area. It's also a big meeting spot in city and has open public plaza on the non-market days*

FUN STUFF

Quad Cinema (indie movie theater w/arthouse films, w13th/5th)
[34 W 13th St] *clean, comfortable small theater playing indie and arthouse films, not state of art or cheap but still another indie theater option in the city, no reserve tickets*

Union Square Market (largest NYC greenmarket in plaza, 14th/Broadway)
[Union Sq Plaza] *the largest NYC greenmarket at Union Sq Plaza, market is every M, W, F & Sat (8am-6pm) - farm fresh produce, eats w/benches & tables in middle park area*

ATTRACTIONS

Union Square Market (largest NYC greenmarket in plaza, 14th/Broadway)
[Union Sq Plaza] *the largest NYC greenmarket at Union Sq Plaza, market is every M, W, F & Sat (8am-6pm) - farm fresh produce, eats w/benches & tables in middle park area*

The Strand Bookstore (famous large used bookstore in NYC, Broadway/e12th)
[828 Broadway] *beloved used bookstore in a huge space w/three levels of rare books, art books & used books, $1 book sales on sidewalk, iconic destination for book lovers*

SOHO
Soho West, Nolita, Little Italy, Noho

quick directions

Soho - Nolita, Little Italy, Noho
Take R, W downtown to Prince St stop [Prince/Broadway]

(or)

Soho West
(by Sullivan St, Varick St, Hudson St)
Take C, E downtown to Spring St stop [Spring/6th Ave]

COFFEE

Now or Never Coffee (cheerful & stylish coffee shop, Grand/Thompson)
[30 Grand St.] *friendly relaxed coffee spot in a warm industrial loft space w/leafy walls, couches, tables, bookshelves & sunlit open-paned window front, serving coffee, espressos, mocha flat whites, pastries, breakfast sandwiches and good vibes, Wifi*

787 Coffee (upbeat cafe serving Puerto Rican coffee & pastries, Thompson/Spring)
[72 Thompson St.] *[72 Thompson St.] cozy & energetic cafe serving coffee drinks from beans sourced from Puerto Rico, Spanish pastries, empanadas & specialty lattes like Marzipan (nut-based) lattes*

Ground Support Cafe (neighborhood coffee shop, W.Broadway/Spring)
[399 W Broadway] *coffee shop in center of Soho with a big space and natural light, food and pastry w/seating at picnic tables & wood benches, Wifi*

L.A. Burdick Handmade Chocolate (chocolate shop w/hot chocolate, desserts, Prince/Thompson)
[156 Prince St] *chocolate and dessert shop by Swiss-trained chocolatier Larry Burdick w/tables inside serving their own special hot chocolate, coffee & chocolate desserts in a European wood-styled setting (no bathroom, no Wifi)*

Housing Works Bookstore & Cafe (cafe, used bookstore & event space, Crosby/Prince)
[126 Crosby St] *cafe in a big used bookstore and event space by Housing Works (which runs a great chain of thrift stores in city), enormous store for Soho w/plenty of seating & tables,winding staircases to the upstairs level and plenty of books, serves coffee, food & drinks, all profits go to charitable mission behind it, can host big events, Wifi*

La Colombe Coffee Roasters (coffee shop in Hudson Sq, VanDam/Hudson)
[75 Vandam St] *roomy and spacious coffee shop from upscale and stylish coffee chain in Hudson Sq with long tables & benches in loft space (no Wifi)*

Maman Soho (gourmet French American cafe & bakery, Centre/Grand)
[239 Centre St] *stylish French American cafe with an elegant gourmet aesthetic, breakfast, brunch & bakery in industrial rustic Soho space (no Wifi)*

Gasoline Alley Coffee (coffee shop in Noho, Lafayette/Bleeker)
[325 Lafayette St] *Noho coffee shop in interesting location with street views on either side, serves Intelligentsia coffee, pastry w/limited seating, grab & go (no bathroom, no Wifi)*

Saturdays NYC (cafe in surf store w/patio deck, Crosby/Grand)
[31 Crosby St] *laid back surf store in a unique Soho space with a coffee stand and patio deck garden in back to relax in, Wifi*

TEA

Harney & Sons Soho (tea room & store, Broome/Broadway)
[433 Broome St] *popular tea store that sounds royal and English but actually started in Connecticut with a nice rustic tea room in back serving pots of tea w/sets of pastries & scones*

The Chai Spot (chai tea place & exotic hangout spot, Mott/Broome)
[156 Mott St] *unique chai tea cafe experience & hangout spot in Soho, inspired by Pakistani colors, flavors & textures in a strikingly colorful space w/decorated pillows and lounge cushions to get comfy in and relax with chai lattes, cardamom teas, samosas & snacks, also has events*

Matchaful (elegant & roomy matcha tea cafe, Prince/Sullivan)
[184 Prince St] *matcha cafe in a long hall-like space with liesurely & table seating, serving chai lattes, teas, pastries, desserts & vegan matcha soft-serve ice cream*

EATS

($)

Prince Street Pizza (old school square pizza slice, Prince/Mott)
[27 Prince St] *old school square slice on many top NYC pizza slice lists, especially its popular pepperoni slice w/limited seating, more for takeout to street, can get busy*

Eileen's Special Cheesecake (beloved cheesecake shop, ClevelandPlace/Spring)
[17 Cleveland Pl] *original, beloved old NY shop of Eileen's cheesecake, serves cheesecake of the light & fluffy variety w/seating in a small shop space*

Sunrise Mart (Japanese market & eats, Broome/W.Broadway)
[494 Broome St] *Japanese supermarket with ready-to-eat prepared foods, rice balls, bento boxes, drinks w/seating & dining space in front*

Saigon Vietnamese Sandwich Deli (banh mi sandwich, Broome/Mott)
[369 Broome St] *Vietnamese banh mi sandwich, popular "#1 sandwich", well regarded & inexpensive, more for grab & go, cash only!*

Chobani Cafe Soho (yogurt & snack cafe, Prince/W.Broadway)
[152 Prince St] *snack cafe in Soho by Chobani Greek yogurt, serves coffee, parfait cups, yogurt drinks, gourmet eats & snacks w/limited seating*

Taïm Mediterranean Kitchen - Nolita (vegan casual eats in corner spot, Spring/Mulberry)
[45 Spring St] *veggie fast casual chain, falafel sandwiches & salads w/limited seating*

Trader Joe's Soho (groceries & organic foods, take A, C train to Spring St. Station with TJ's above it, Spring St/6th Ave)
[233 Spring Street] *one of the best Trader Joe's in the city, roomy store in a big easy-to-shop-in space, perfect for lunches and eats, easy to get to for visitors and locals since it's above a train stop w/utensils for grab & go at exit, can eat at park area outside with patio tables & benches*

($$)

Alidoro (Italian specialty sandwich shop, est. 1896, Sullivan/Spring)
[105 Sullivan St] *authentic Italian gourmet sandwiches at original shop location w/limited seating, highly regarded & popular, grab & go, cash only!*

Parisi Bakery & Delicatessen (authentic Italian sandwiches, Mott/Kenmare)
[198 Mott St] *old-time bakery establishment that serves large, high quality Italian meat sandwiches, popular w/locals & well regarded, grab & go with no seating, cash only!*

Maman Soho (gourmet French American cafe & bakery, Centre/Grand)
[239 Centre St] *stylish French American cafe with an elegant gourmet aesthetic, breakfast, brunch, bakery in industrial rustic Soho space*

Black Tap Craft Burgers & Beer (burger place w/Crazy Milkshakes, Broome/Sullivan)
[529 Broome St] *very popular, fun take on classic NYC burger joint w/craft burgers, craft beer & over-the-top, huge "Crazy Milkshakes", fun & lively burger experience, can have long lines*

The Grey Dog Nolita (cafe/restaurant, American comfort food, Mulberry/Prince)
[244 Mulberry St] *cozy rustic place with American comfort food, better for breakfast or lunch w/seating, Wifi, popular*

Balthazar Boulangerie (small French bakery, Spring/Broadway)
[80 Spring St] *charming French boulangerie next to main Balthazar restaurant - croissants, sandwiches, pastries, cakes, no seating, has benches outside, well regarded, grab & go*

Dominique Ansel Bakery (French bakery, home of the "cronut", Spring/Sullivan)
[189 Spring St] *French bakery & dessert shop, home of the famous "cronut" (donut/croissant) w/food, pastries with seating, patio garden, often has lines for the cronut, popular*

Despaña (Spanish sandwiches, tapas, market, Broome/Lafayette)
[408 Broome St] *sandwich place & gourmet market w/meats from Spain - prosciutto, chorizo, tapas, highly-rated sandwiches, w/seating*

Rubirosa Ristorante (Italian thin crust pizza restaurant, Mulberry/Prince)
[235 Mulberry St] *Italian restaurant with thin crust pizza and authentic cuisine, lively atmosphere, highly-rated for best NYC pizza w/tables & bar seating*

Morgenstern's Finest Ice Cream (artisanal small-batch ice cream in Soho style, like Salted Pretzel Caramel, Blueberry Milk Chocolate, wHouston/wBroadway)
[88 W Houston St] *gourmet ice cream parlor with 88 flavors of artisanal ingredients*

and inventive textures like Salted Pretzel Caramel, Blueberry Milk Chocolate &
Vietnamese Coffee in a reimagined throwback long-spaced parlor w/tables outside,
also serves gourmet takes on comfort food classics- burger, pies, milkshakes & desserts

($$$)

Balthazar (famous Soho French bistro restaurant, Spring/Crosby)
[80 Spring St] *probably the most famous restaurant in Soho, a destination French bistro*
restaurant since 1980's, serves French comfort food, steak frites, fries, brunch. Big, bustling
& trendy in a spacious and roomy restaurant interior w/its boulangerie bakery next door

Blue Ribbon Sushi (famous sushi place, Sullivan/Prince)
[119 Sullivan St] *famous sushi restaurant w/blue ribbon special, omakase, well regarded*
and popular, no reservations, wait/walk-in only

DRINKS & BARS

($)

Botanica Bar (dive bar, E.Houston/Mott)
[47 E Houston St] *dimly-lit dive bar in underground space w/cheap beers, loud music,*
can be laid back or raucous, w/DJ nights

($$)

Ear Inn (old time NYC tavern, city landmark, Spring/Greenwich)
[326 Spring St] *est. 1817, one of oldest bars in NYC, good-sized place that's a designated*
landmark w/Ear Inn Ale, decent pub food, a big ear sculpture on wall & Sunday jazz nights

Spring Lounge (laid back dive bar, Spring/Mulberry)
[8 Spring St] *laid back, rustic wood-planked dive bar decorated w/sharks, the bar looks out into*
cinematic street views of Soho, just drinks but on Wed nights after 5, often gives out free hot dogs

Fanelli's Cafe (old time NYC gastropub, Prince/Mercer)
[94 Prince St] *bar in the heart of Soho that's straight out of a Scorcese movie with old*
time NYC ambience, decent food and plenty of atmosphere

Mother's Ruin (cocktails/beers, comfort food, Spring/Elizabeth)
[18 Spring St] *low-key, spacious neighborhood bar with good food and Soho vibe,*
serves french onion soup grilled cheese, waffle fries, slushy drinks in comfortable space

SHOPPING

Shopping in Soho

[on Broadway] - *Muji, Bloomingdale's Soho, Uniqlo, Pearl River Mart & various shops*

[on Mott St, btw Prince & West Houston] - *about one block of downtown-style specialty boutique stores for cosmetics, shoes, gifts, few more in surrounding area*

[in Soho West, btw Broadway & West Broadway] - *downtown branches of uptown stores, luxury and designer brands, Apple Soho store, scattered around Prince & Spring streets inside ironwork storefronts and former art galleries*

[on Canal St, & Broadway] - *street shopping w/sidewalk vendors on Canal St by Chinatown*

- - - -

Bloomingdale's Soho (upscale department store, Broadway/Spring)
[504 Broadway] *multileveled downtown store of Bloomingdale's main store with contemporary & urban focused clothes, clean/free restrooms in basement-handy in Soho*

McNally Jackson Books (independent bookstore, Prince/West Broadway)
[134 Prince St] *dynamic and well-ordered indie bookstore, a bedrock of the neighborhood that's comfy to browse w/fine selection of books from classics to contemporary*

Muji Soho (Japanese items, clothes, Broadway/Grand)
[455 Broadway] *Japanese clothing & house items store with tasteful and elegant products, office and art supplies, leans towards minimalist design w/tan, off-white & mute colors*

Uniqlo Soho (Japanese clothing, Broadway/Spring)
[546 Broadway] *major clothing brand in Japan, affordable & stylish clothes in large location*

Pearl River Mart (Chinese gifts, home goods store, Broadway/Grand)
[452 Broadway] *newer, more compact version of the used-to-be larger Pearl River store with Chinese house goods, decorations & gifts*

Patagonia (eco-friendly, outdoor clothing & gear, Greene/Spring)
[72 Greene St] *three floors of high quality outdoor clothing, fleece jackets, coats, camping gear, hiking gear & accessories by Patagonia, a brand known for its eco-friendly products, w/repair center in basement of a nicely remodeled Soho building that was originally built in 1872*

Sample Sales in Soho
[Soho] *Many sample sales take place in the Soho area. Sample sales are usually high-end brands and designer merchandise that sell their overstock at marked down prices at a pop up store address for a week or so. Those in the know shop this way to get better sales and cheaper deals on nicer stuff, especially from the high end brands. Blogs, social media & Instagrams are good ways to keep track of the best sample sales in the city —from clothes, jackets, handbags, hats, backpacks to stationary supplies, kitchen & house items*

FUN STUFF & ATTRACTIONS

Shopping in Soho
[on Broadway] - *Muji, Bloomingdale's Soho, Uniqlo, Pearl River and various shops*
[on Mott St, btw Prince & West Houston] - *downtown specialty & boutique stores*
[in Soho West, btw Broadway & West Broadway] - *luxury & designer brands, Apple Soho*
[on Canal St, & Broadway] - *street shopping w/ sidewalk vendors on Canal St by Chinatown*

Angelika Film Center & Cafe (indie, classic, art movies, W.Houston/Broadway)
[18 W Houston St] *one of oldest indie movies theaters in business with 5 small theaters, large and roomy outside waiting area in with a cafe & patio table seating*

Museum of Ice Cream (museum w/playful fun rooms celebrating ice cream, W.Houston/Broadway)
[558 Broadway] *Not an educational museum but more a self-tour through themed fun rooms celebrating all things ice cream (& selfie photos) often served ice cream, kid friendly, pricey*

The Basilica of St. Patrick's Old Cathedral (historic site, Mulberry/Mott)
[263 Mulberry St] *gothic church in Nolita that's oldest catholic church in the city, built in 1809 w/19th century architecture, has catacombs below available for tours, offers Sunday masses in 4 languages*

Walking Tours of Little Italy & Chinatown
[166 Walker St, Official Information Kiosk at triangle of Walker, Baxter & Canal St in Chinatown] *open daily from 10am- 6pm, usually has staff to give info about NYC attractions and walking tours to enjoy the next door areas of Little Italy & Chinatown, offers guided walking tours that takes you around the best of these neighborhoods*

CHINATOWN

quick directions
Take 6, N, Q, W, R, J, Z downtown to Canal St stop [Canal/Broadway]

COFFEE

Little Canal (coffee shop, roomy cafe, bar at night, Canal/Essex)
[26 Canal St] *solid, comfortable cafe/bar in Chinatown, food, baked goods from Balthazar w/seating in a cozy & roomy space (no laptops, no Wifi)*

Blue Bottle Coffee (cafe in lobby of Walker Hotel, Broadway/Walker St)
[396 Broadway] *SF coffee roaster chain near Canal St in a fancy ironwork-styled hotel with comfortable window seating, pour over coffee, pastries, Wifi*

Dreamers Coffee House (quaint little coffee shop, Henry/Market St)
[54 W Henry] *intimate neighborhood coffee shop on a quiet street, serves lattes, mochas, espressos, pastries w/ limited seating, Wifi (no bathroom)*

CHINATOWN

TEA

Yaya Tea (tea cafe, bubble teas, homemade rice balls, Chrystie/Canal)
[51 Chrystie St] *tea cafe specializing in hot & cold teas, bubble teas, homemade specialty rice balls w/seating & table space*

Alimama Tea & Dessert (tea cafe w/mochi donuts, cream puffs, Bayard/Mulberry)
[89A Bayard St] *dessert shop in Chinatown specializing in mochi donuts, cream puffs and pastries as well as teas, bubble teas & milk teas, limited counter seating*

Kettl Tea (japanese matcha tea stand in Bowery Mkt, Bowery/GreatJonesSt)
[348 Bowery] *cute tea stand at the outdoor Bowery Market selling authentic Japanese matcha tea, matcha lattes & tea desserts like matcha gelato, has small side tables*

EATS

($)

Scarr's Pizza (highly-rated pizza slice, Orchard/Canal)
[35 Orchard St] *highly-rated NYC slice that's on many best of NY lists in a new storefront with more space for selling slices now (used to be in authentic 70's diner space that had a fun retro décor but perhaps hard for all the business this very popular slice brings in)*

Nom Wah Tea Parlor (popular dim sum, Doyers/Bowery)
[13 Doyers St] *oldest &most popular dim sum in NYC with old school 1920's interior, always on top of NY dim sum lists, affordable w/seating*

Original Chinatown Ice Cream Factory (ice cream parlor, Bayard/Mott)
[65 Bayard St] *family-owned business w/generously-sized handmade ice cream scoops in inventive flavors, black sesame ice cream, always on NYC best lists, no seating, grab & go*

Saigon Vietnamese Sandwich Deli (banh mi sandwich, Broome/Mott)
[369 Broome St] *Vietnamese banh mi sandwich, popular "#1 sandwich", well regarded & inexpensive, more for grab & go, cash only!*

Xi'an Famous Foods (Chinese noodles, Bayard/Bowery)
[45 Bayard St] *NYC chain of western Chinese cuisine, hand-ripped noodle dishes in roomy space w/seating*

Noodle Village (Cantonese, wanton/congee soups, Mott/Mosco)
[13 Mott St] *popular restaurant in Chinatown with wanton and congee soups, hot pots, noodle dishes & soup dumplings*

Super Taste (Taiwanese noodle soups, Eldridge/Canal)
[26 Eldridge St] *small no-frills Taiwanese restaurant specializing in noodle soups, hand cut noodles, known for being spicy, good & cheap*

Great N.Y. Noodletown (Chinese roast duck, roast pork, Bowery/Bayard)
[28 Bowery] *place to go for Chinese roast duck, roast pork & in-season soft shell crabs, favorite of chefs for late night eats*

($$)

Canal Street Market (urban food hall in Chinatown, Canal St/Cortland Alley)
[265 Canal St] *Asian-focused food hall in modern industrial space w/food stands - Chinatown Deli, Lazy Sundaes , Joe's Steam Rice Roll, Enzo Bruni La Pizza Gourmet & Betong Thai w/nice bathrooms, good seating & Wifi*

Shanghai 21 (soup dumplings, Mott/Mosco)
[21 Mott St] *Shanghainese style noodle bowls, well-regarded soup dumplings, dim sum, popular & gets crowded, cash/amex only!*

Joe's Shanghai (famous soup dumplings, Bowery/Canal St)
[46 Bowery St] *world famous soup dumplings, always on top dim sum lists in NYC w/big shared round tables and other seating, popular & gets crowded, foodie destination*

DRINKS & BARS

($)

Forgtmenot (dive bar w/food, Division/Canal)
[138 Division St] *eclectic and laid back small bar that's a good meetup place, serves food, breakfast tacos in a warm and cozy setting*

($$)

Clandestino (casual neighborhood bar, Canal/Ludlow)
[35 Canal St] *solid neighborhood place, laid back bar that's softy lit and comfortable*

CHINATOWN

Whiskey Tavern (laid back, saloon-style neighborhood tavern, Baxter/White)
[79 Baxter St] *popular downtown tavern near the city courts known for being relaxed w/solid pub food, booths & nice-sized patio garden space in back w/good happy hour specials*

($$$)
Apothéke (famous & fancy cocktail bar, Doyers/Pell)
[9 Doyers St] *famous speakeasy cocktail bar housed in what used to be an opium den, dark and luxurious, live jazz nights, pricey*

The Crown (rooftop bar on top of Hotel 50, Bowery/Canal)
[50 Bowery] *roof deck and bar on top of Hotel 50 with indoor lounge, outdoor lounge and couches that look onto sweeping views of Manhattan & Brooklyn Bridge*

SHOPPING, FUN STUFF & ATTRACTIONS

Walking Tours of Little Italy & Chinatown
[166 Walker St, Official Information Kiosk at triangle of Walker, Baxter & Canal St in Chinatown] *open daily from 10am- 6pm, usually has staff to give info about NYC attractions and walking tours to enjoy the next door areas of Little Italy & Chinatown, offers guided walking tours that takes you around the best of these neighborhoods*

Metrograph (indie movies, old & new, art house w/bar upstairs. Ludlow/Canal)
[7 Ludlow St] *stylish arthouse and indie movie theater with lounge area and bar upstairs, everything is designed with retro elegance from snacks to theater signs*

Original Chinatown Ice Cream Factory (ice cream parlor, Bayard/Mott)
[65 Bayard St] *family-owned business w/generously-sized handmade ice cream scoops in inventive flavors, black sesame ice cream, always on NYC best lists, no seating, grab & go*

Shopping on Canal St (all along Canal St, Canal/Broadway)
[Canal St near Broadway] *street shopping from sidewalk vendors on Canal St to buy clothing and often imitation copies of brand name purses, wallets, bags & accessories*

LOWER EAST SIDE
East Village, St. Marks Place

quick directions

East Village / St. Marks Place / Astor Place
(by NYU, St. Marks Place)
Take 4, 5, 6 downtown to Astor Place stop [e8th/Lafayette]

(or)

Lower East Side (LES)
(Bowery, E. Houston St, Alphabet City, Tompkins Sq Pk)
Take F downtown to 2nd Ave Station stop [E.Houston/Allen]

(or)

Lower East Side (LES)
(Essex St, Clinton St, Orchard St, Rivington St, Stanton St)
Take F downtown to Delancey St/Essex St stop [Delancey/Essex]

COFFEE

Abraço (atmospheric saloon-style cafe w/comfort & style, e7th/1st)
[86 E 7th St] *open & easygoing cafe in a lounge setting with drinks served from a coffee bar along with baked goods, cortados & ambience, w/table benches & chairs (no Wifi)*

The Granddaddy (roomy & cozy hangout LES coffeeshop, Grand/Eldridge)
[290 Grand St] *roomy coffeeshop with a modern, large-windowed inviting corner space shop with a generous amount of seating for the laptop and hangout crowd, serves signature toasted black sesame lattes, matcha lattes, teas, pastries, beer & wine at night, Wifi*

Ludlow Coffee Supply (roomy coffee shop, Ludlow/E.Houston)
[176 Ludlow St] *big coffee shop in downtown industrial space that's roomy & easy to lounge in, w/coffee, food and pastries, vintage chairs & couches in a few rooms, popular, Wifi*

Caffe Vita Coffee Roasting Co. (coffee shop, Ludlow/Rivington)
[124 Ludlow St] *small cafe of respected Seattle roaster, dark wooded, brick interior with cool looking coffee grinder in back w/limited seating, grab & go, Wifi*

Black Cat LES (cozy big coffee shop, Rivington/Clinton)
[172 Rivington St] *lower-level, generously sized coffee lounge that's cozy and chill, roomy to work in, serving coffee, food, pastry and bagels booths, hanging lights, w/ mixed furniture, spacious and eclectic clubhouse vibe in city, Wifi*

OST Cafe (coffee shop, roomy inside, Grand/E.Broadway)
[511 Grand St] *quaint, mid-sized coffee shop with plants in a nice space, espressos, pastries in a less trafficked area w/seating, Wifi*

Ninth Street Espresso (coffee shop by Tompkins Sq Park, e10th/AveB)
[341 E 10th St] *coffee shop in a minimalist long hall space, serves espressos with wall & window seating across from Tompkins Sq Park with views of park, Wifi (no bathroom)*

C&B Cafe (cafe across from Tompkins Sq Pk, breakfast sandwich, e7th/Ave B)
[178 E 7th St] *cafe, breakfast/lunch spot across from Tompkins Sq Park with high-rated chorizo and egg breakfast sandwich, well maintained with good food, artsy touches w/table seating area in back, Wifi*

Elsewhere Espresso (quaint coffee shop, cookies, e6th/1stAve)
[335 E 6th St] *sunny, chill out mid-sized coffee shop with red storefront, espressos, cookies, pastries in well ordered space w/seating & bench outside, Wifi*

Saltwater Coffee (stylish & sunny Australian coffee shop, e12th/1stAve)
[345 E 12th St] *small cafe with stylish & bright decor serving Australian coffee, flat whites, matcha lattes, turmeric lattes & pastries w/few tables in a relaxing space, Wifi (no bathrooms)*

TEA

Cha-An Teahouse (Japanese tea house near St. Marks Place, e9th/2nd)
[230 E 9th St Fl 2] *upstairs Japanese tea house in St Marks Place area, serene Japanese style tea rooms with good food, fancy desserts and tea sets, pleasant escape from the city into a warm atmospheric setting, highly-rated & well regarded*

Hi-Collar (Japanese cafe, tea & sake bar, e10th/1st)
[214 E 10th St] *Japanese cafe and tea place w/fluffy hot cakes & siphon coffee, lunch, omurice, katsu sandwiches, sake bar at night in art nouveau space*

Teado Tea Shop (Taiwanese bubble tea shop, Hester/Bowery)
[145D Hester St] *small Taiwanese bubble tea shop, makes custom bubble tea, with limited seating, bench outside, more grab & go*

Debutea (Taiwanese-style bubble & fruit tea shop, Thompson/3rd)
[217 Thompson St] *Counter service boba tea & high-quality fruit tea shop w/signature fruit teas like Coco Mango, inviting décor, few tables inside, benches outside, popular*

Setsugekka East Village (japanese matcha tea house, e7th/1st)
[74 E 7th St] *serene, elegant Japanese matcha tea house in small tatami room-like space, serving matcha desserts & house made matcha with tea sets & tea ceremonies at counter with an old-time macha-making device*

EATS

($)

Scarr's Pizza (highly-rated pizza slice, Orchard/Canal)
[35 Orchard St] *highly-rated NYC slice that's on many best of NY lists in a new storefront with more space for selling slices now (used to be in authentic 70's diner space that had a fun retro décor but perhaps hard for all the business this very popular slice brings in)*

Vanessa's Dumpling House (good and cheap dumplings, Eldridge/Broome)
[118A Eldridge St] *Chinese dumpling house in LES with seating and bench tables full of people making the trek to eat here, can eat a lot for a small price, inexpensive and highly rated, popular & crowded*

7th St Burger (original location of popular smashburger NYC chain, e7th/1stAve)
[91 East 7th St] *original NYC cheeseburger spot of chain that's taken off in the city with its affordable Smash Burger, fries & simple menu, small place w/a few tables outside*

Joey Bats Cafe (bakery cafe w/Portuguese custard flaky tarts, Allen/Kenmare)
[129 Allen St] *quaint Portuguese bakery cafe w/Pasteis de Natas specialty, natas are like a croissant tart filled with warm custard cream, baked all day w/limited seating*

Wah Fung No. 1 (Cantonese barbecue rice platters w/roast pork, roast duck, roast chicken, Chrystie/Hester)
[79 Chrystie St] *can easily find this popular small red shop with hanging barbeque meats in the window by looking for the long lines outside, serves inexpensive rice platters of roast pork, roast duck or roast chicken, grab & go (can take meal to park across street)*

Sunny & Annie's Deli (bodega sandwiches, well regarded, AveB/6th)
[94 Avenue B] *no-frills deli that's famous with foodies and locals for its range of well made, inventive and generous-sized bodega sandwiches with colorful names, each one has a detailed description on the decorative signs at the front, well regarded & inexpensive, open late night, no seating, just grab & go*

Creperie (French crepes, counter service to order, Ludlow/Rivington)
[135 Ludlow St] *gourmet French crepes in atmospheric nook on Ludlow St, serving sweet & savory crepes, made-to-order w/minimal seating, open late night, grab & go*

Bel-Fries (Belgian french fries, counter service to order, Ludlow/Rivington)
[132 Ludlow St] *small counter shop that opens out to sidewalk that specializes in made-from-scratch Belgian fries w/sauces, served in in 3 sizes of paper cones, grab & go*

Xe Máy Sandwich Shop (Vietnamese bánh mi sandwich, 1stAve/StMarks)
[96 St. Marks Pl] *small Vietnamese sandwich shop, serving its popular bánh mi sub sandwich w/limited wall seating, grab & go*

($$)

Clinton St. Baking Co. (famous breakfast & brunch place, Clinton/E.Houston)
[4 Clinton St] *renown gourmet breakfast and brunch spot that's a foodie destination, known for its blueberry pancakes & waffles, serves brunch comfort food with farm fresh ingredients in a corner diner space w/plenty of seating, well known & highly regarded*

Cocoron (Japanese soba noodle restaurant, Delancey/Chrystie)
[16 Delancey St] *Japanese soba place with homemade soba noodles with a vegetarian focus & health conscious, good space w/seating in warm-toned interior, highly regarded, cash only!*

Flippers (popular Japanese soufflé pancake house, wBroadway/Grand)
[337 W. Broadway] *downtown pancake house specializing in Japanese soufflé pancakes (a fluffy, light pancake) w/sweet & savory options like Signature Flippers Souffle, Matcha Flippers pancakes with comfort food, desserts in comfortable modern 2nd floor dining space, popular so it can get crowded w/waits*

Motorino (brick oven pizza, e12th/1st)
[349 E 12th St] *mid-sized Brooklyn-based brick oven pizzeria, often on best of NY pizza pie list, gourmet pies, buffalo mozzarella w/seating, well regarded*

Ivan Ramen (popular & well regarded LES ramen place, Clinton/Stanton)
[25 Clinton St] *very popular ramen place in LES with reasonable prices in long counter hall space lined with tables, also has quality appetizers & desserts w/garden seating in back, usually has lines*

Mighty Quinn's BBQ (bbq & brisket joint, 2nd/e6th)
[103 2nd Ave] *slow-smoked bbq place amongst best in city, a fast casual chain of bbq places serving brisket, burnt ends, side fixings, roomy space with earthy-rustic décor, long tables for seating for the downtown bbq experience, well regarded*

Hi-Collar (Japanese cafe, tea & sake bar, e10th/1st)
[214 E 10th St] *Japanese cafe and tea place w/fluffy hot cakes & siphon coffee, lunch, omurice, katsu sandwiches, sake bar at night in art nouveau space*

Lil' Frankies (Italian brick oven pizzeria, e1st/1st)
[19 1st Ave] *Naples-style brick oven Italian pizzeria that serves Italian comfort food dishes, pasta w/close quarter seating, bar area, opens up to street, cash only!*

Russ & Daughters (famous old-time NYC smoked fish, caviar & gourmet specialty shop, E.Houston/1stAve)
[179 E Houston St] *family-owned since 1914, famous NYC bagel smoked fish & gourmet specialty food shop with Scottish smoked salmon, cream cheese, bagels & lox, caviar, reasonable to pricey, foodie destination so can get busy, grab & go with benches outside (also has a sit-down restaurant nearby w/tables @127 Orchard St)*

Bobwhite Counter (fried chicken, soul food, Ave C/e6th)
[94 Avenue C] *LES lunch and supper counter serving soul food in festive old-wood lunch counter environment, fried chicken dishes and southern fare with well-made sides, wedge fries, coleslaw, macaroni & cheese w/seating*

The Orchard Grocer (veggie grocer & deli, vegan sandwiches, Orchard/Broome)
[78 Orchard St] *veggie-focused deli and grocer, vegan deli sandwiches, vegan soft serve ice cream, vegan bakery, vegan groceries w/ few window seats, grab & go*

Levain Bakery Noho (downtown shop of famous UWS bakery known for its cookies, Lafayette/Bleecker)
[340 Lafayette St] *downtown branch of famous UWS bakery known for its chunky chocolate chip cookies considered best in the city (esp. chocolate chip walnut) Also has baked goods, breads, scones and muffins, more set up for grab & go*

Doughnut Plant (donut bakery cafe, Grand/Essex St)
[379 Grand St] *well regarded doughnut bakery with limited seating - coffee, espressos, lattes, unique cake donuts, yeast donuts & specialty donuts, popular, WiFi*

Van Leeuwen Ice Cream Shop (gourmet ice cream shop w/vegan flavors, e7th/2nd)
[48 ½ E 7th St] *gourmet ice cream w/vegan ice cream, shakes, sundaes and flavors like Earl Grey Tea, in fairly large windowed space w/retro vibe, counter window seating & tables*

Essex Market (market & urban food hall, Essex/Delancey)
[88 Essex St] *newly renovated urban food hall in LES Essex Street Market in a modern industrial space featuring local style food - Shopsin's (comfort food), Don Ceviche (Peruvian rotisserie chicken), Top Hops (craft beer bar) w/ cheese & fruit stands, seating and more eateries downstairs, also next to a new downtown movie theater complex*

Whole Foods Bowery (eats, tables, food stands & lounge upstairs , E.Houston/Bowery)
[95 E Houston St] *Whole Foods Market has a huge 2nd floor eating and lounge area w/plenty of seating, tables and couches where you can bring your hot food, eats or coffee upstairs or order from its food stands, w/bathrooms & Wifi*

($$-$$$)

Katz's Delicatessen (est. 1888, classic old-time NYC deli & Jewish restaurant, famous for its giant sandwiches, E.Hudson/Ludlow)
[205 E Houston St] *classic NYC institution, NYC's oldest deli on the Lower East Side serving "mile high sandwiches" like Pastrami and Rueben sandwiches, served in the*

original old-timey setting since 1888, plenty of seating, big foodie destination so can get busy, often crowded, pricey but generous size so easy to share (sandwiches @$20-$30)

DRINKS & BARS

($)

McSorley's Old Ale House (old time tavern bar, e7th/3rd)
[15 E 7th St] *est. 1854, a drinking pub of lore and one of the oldest bars in NYC, beers are cheap and come by the pair only - light or dark McSorley's Ale, everything looks like it came from an Americana time portal because it does (Abe Lincoln had drinks here once) crowds are usually festive, inexpensive bar food, an experience, cash only!*

The Magician (dive bar, cheap drinks, Rivington/Essex)
[118 Rivington St] *mellow LES dive bar in an interesting newsroom-like space with diner tables and tiled floors, good for hanging out with cheap beers, happy hours, cash only!*

169 Bar (famous dive bar w/kitschy decor, pool table, E.Broadway/Essex)
[169 E Broadway] *famous dive bar with eclectic vibe, decorated with mermaids, dinosaurs, disco balls with a leopard-print pool table, cheap beers and happy hours, roomy and kitschy, popular place on weekends, better on weeknights*

Ace Bar (dive bar w/skee-ball, pinball, pool tables & darts, e5th/AveA)
[531 E 5th St] *casual and fun dive bar, dimly lit with lounge booths all around w/art nouveau window frames outside, cheap beers and happy hours w/skee-ball, pool tables, pinball machines & darts, can browse their vintage lunchbox collection*

Doc Holliday's (dive bar w/pool table, across from Tompkins Sq Park, AveA/e9th)
[141 Avenue A] *dive bar in heart of Alphabet City covered with western murals outside, cheap beer, jukebox, video game and a pool table; can get raucous, fun and loud but also can be mellow and laid back, depends on the time*

($$)

Antler (craft beer basement bar, Allen/Delancey)
[123 Allen St] *warm and cozy rustic basement bar in long space with craft beer and wine, w/roomy back area & couches, happy hour specials*

Kingston Hall (casual bar & lounge w/pool tables, 2nd/9th)
[149 2nd Ave] *casual place on the dive bar side with roomy lounge in an old wood interior w/ working fireplaces, pool tables, Jamaican cocktails & kitschy decorative touches, happy hour specials*

Fool's Gold NYC (craft beer bar & cocktail bar, E.Houston/Eldridge)
[145 E Houston St] *relaxed, casual craft beer and cocktail bar with rustic decor, chicken wings, pub grub and Sunday night bingo, w/skeeball & games in back area*

Swift Hibernian Lounge (cozy Irish tavern bar, e4th/Bowery)
[34 E 4th St] *warm and cozy Irish pub tavern serving pints and food that feels like it was ported over from Dublin, with murals to the writer Jonathan Swift painted on the walls, thick wood interior with scratchy tables, open booths & chunky bar fixtures, happy hours*

($$$)
Hotel Chantelle (rooftop lounge w/jazz music, Ludlow/Delancey)
[92 Ludlow St] *trendy and picturesque rooftop bar with stylish glass roof casing and cocktail lounge on top of a French inspired restaurant complex, serves brunches, comfort foods, stuffed French toast, has weekend jazz brunch with live musicians*

SHOPPING

Casey Rubber Stamps (rubber stamps, e11th/2nd)
[322 E 11th St] *fun artsy shop specializing in rubber stamps, makes their own stamps and custom stamps*

Bonnie Slotnick Cookbooks (cookbook bookstore, e2nd/Bond]
[28 E 2nd St] *quaint independent bookstore specializing in used, vintage & out of print cookbooks, charming, unique & intimate w/backyard patio for reading*

MooShoes NYC (vegan and cruelty-free shoes, Orchard/Broome)
[78 Orchard St] *well put-together store that sells vegan shoes and cruelty-free accessories, wallets, t-shirts, books w/pop-up vegan bake sales*

Astor Wines & Spirits (large LES liquor store & wine shop, Lafayette/e4th)
[399 Lafayette St] *wine store near Astor Place in a good location that is a massive space for a liquor store in NYC, roomy and well ordered with large selection of classic wines, laid out by region - European wines, California wines, sake, spirits*

Small shops & boutique stores scattered throughout LES
[LES] *Bond St, Orchard St, Delancey St, Allen St, Ludlow St, e10th, St Mark's Place*

OUTDOOR PUBLIC SPACES

Tompkins Square Park (city park in Alphabet City, btw Ave A&B, 9th/AveA)
[500 E 9th St] *small park in Alphabet city in the center of LES w/playgrounds, handball court, dog run, chess tables and a basketball court, place to relax and people watch with coffee shops and eateries around it, w/Greenmarket on Sundays from 9-4 p year round*

FUN STUFF

Economy Candy (popular old school NYC candy store, Rivington/Essex)
[108 Rivington St] *fun candy store in business since 1937, might even have the same sign, stocked from floor to ceiling with all kinds of cheap candy, sweets and treats , busy & popular*

Regal Essex Crossing & RPX movie theaters (new movie theater complex above Essex St Mkt, Delancey/Norfolk)
[129 Delancey St] *fancy new movie theater multiplex next to Essex St. Market with 14 theaters, comfy recliner seats, bar space & good sized lounge area w/street views, highly-rated*

Metrograph (indie, old movies & new movies w/bar upstairs, Ludlow/Canal)
[7 Ludlow St] *stylish, independent, arthouse movie theater with comfortable seats and spacious theaters, select snacks, bar lounge area, upstairs bistro, curated films, perfect for dates or those who want to watch movies in artful style*

Ace Bar (dive bar w/skee-ball, pinball, pool tables & darts, e5th/AveA)
[531 E 5th St] *casual and fun dive bar, dimly lit with lounge booths all around with art nouveau window frames outside, cheap beers and happy hours w/skee-ball, pool tables, pinball machines & darts, can browse their vintage lunchbox collection*

MANHATTAN VIEWS

East River Park (river park, btw e14th & Grand, by East River)
[East River Park on FDR Drive] *waterfront park with scenic views of the East River, the Williamsburg Bridge and Manhattan views down river, for walking, running & biking, please note that it might be difficult to get to from LES since it's on the other side of FDR Drive (which is basically a highway around NYC)*

ATTRACTIONS

St. Marks Place (famous festive East Village street walk, 8th/3rd)
[8th St btw 3rd Ave & Ave A] *lively East Village thoroughfare that people stroll through for 3 blocks to experience a food crawl, shopping stores and people watching in a storied part of Greenwich Village/East Village*

Tenement Museum (museum about immigrant experience, Orchard/Delancey)
[103 Orchard St] *highly regarded museum that features an old tenement built in 1860s that's a time capsule showing the immigrant experience from NYC's past in the Lower East Side tenements, specifically the 1860s to the 1930s by preserving the apartments they lived in (@ 97 Orchard St), can take tours of different apartments, also features costumed actors recreating immigrant life and conditions in the apartments, best to book tickets early, popular attraction*

Downtown bars, dive bars, food scene, shops
[LES] *interesting bars and restaurants around neighborhood with a distinct downtown style about them. LES has a variety of specialty and food shops that differentiate it from the rest of Manhattan with a downtown aesthetic that's more artsy, specialized and particular with a bit of retro added to the mix.*

WEST VILLAGE
Greenwich Village, Hudson St

quick directions

West Village
(Greenwich Village, Hudson River Park)
Take 1 downtown to Christopher St stop [Christopher/7thAveSouth]

(or)

Greenwich Village
(Washington Sq Park, NYU)
Take A, B, C, D, E, F, M downtown to W 4th St stop [w14th/8thAve]

COFFEE

Cafe Panino Mucho Gusto (rustic cafe, breakfast, paninis, Hudson/Charles)
[551 Hudson St] *super cozy West Village cafe with all-natural charm that could pass for a cafe in Provence, quaint, light-filled and laid back; full of homey and country furniture, known for its paninis & breakfast w/seating & tables, Wifi*

Caffe Reggio (old world NYC coffee shop, MacDougal/w3rd)
[119 MacDougal St] *est. 1927, "home of original cappuccino", old world cafe with good cappuccinos & desserts, tiny tables w/NYC's first espresso machine on display, old painting, lots of ambience, open till 3AM, Wifi*

The Elk (popular Village cafe, Charles/Greenwich)
[128 Charles St] *urban, mid-sized modern cafe with wood interior inspired by Pacific Northwest, serves SF Sightglass coffee, pastries, food w/seating, popular, Wifi*

Interlude Coffee & Tea (coffee shop, Hudson/Hubert)
[145 Hudson St] *coffee shop with minimalist, sleek white interior, serves coffee, matcha lattes, tea and pastries in a light-filled open space w/seating & tables, a local favorite, Wifi*

Joe Coffee Company (cafe w/patio area, WaverlyPl/GaySt)
[141 Waverly Place] *quaint mid-sized coffee shop in a nicely set up space, part of a reliable NY coffee chain, pastry, donuts w/seating & people-watching bench area outside (no Wifi)*

Partners Coffee (corner coffee shop, CharlesSt/w7th)
[44 Charles St] *coffee shop in triangular corner building space, centrally located with big windows and nice light in a rustic chic interior, serves coffee & pastries, Wifi*

Birch Coffee (coffee shop, 7th/w14th)
[56 7th Ave] *small Birch coffee shop outpost that serves coffee & Dough pastries, chunky wood interior & bookshelves w/limited seating in a cozy space, (no Wifi, no bathroom)*

Stumptown Coffee Roasters (roomy coffee corner shop, w8th/MacDougal)
[30 W 8th St] *flagship NY store of Stumptown Coffee Roasters in good looking corner store space, serves Stumptown coffee and pastries in stylish brick wood interior, roomy hangout space with seating & tables, Wifi*

TEA

McNulty's Tea & Coffee Co. (old time tea shop, Christopher/Bleecker)
[109 Christopher St] *"Rare teas & fine coffees since 1895", perhaps the oldest NYC tea shop that's an institution in the West Village with large variety of jars of teas, tea blends & coffees*

Tea & Sympathy (tea room & British restaurant, Greenwich/Jane)
[108 Greenwich Ave] *British tea room with inn decor that celebrates all things British, serves afternoon tea & crumpets, English comfort food w/table seating*

Té Company (Taiwanese tea room, w10th/7thS)
[163 W 10th St] *intimate Taiwanese tea room in brownstone apartment storefront, serves Taiwanese tea and snacks, meditative & cozy w/limited seating*

EATS

($)

Bleecker Street Pizza (classic NYC pizza place, 7thS/Bleecker)
[69 7th Ave S] *classic NY neighborhood pizza shop on Bleecker St, highly-regarded slice with a firm, thin crust w/seating and sidewalk patio area, popular*

Joe's Pizza (famous NYC slice to go, Carmine/6th)
[7 Carmine St] *small bustling shop with popular slice that's on every best slice of NY list, reliably good with limited seating, can get busy, grab & go, most take slice outside, cash only!*

Mamoun's Falafel (falafel, cheap eats by Wash Sq Park, MacDougal/w3rd)
[119 MacDougal St] *popular small falafel shop by Washington Sq Park, known for being good and cheap, favorite of NYU students, limited seating, more grab & go, cash only!*

Pommes Frites (Belgian fries shop, MacDougal/w3rd)
[128 MacDougal St] *authentic Belgian Fries shop, has over 30 different sauces to go with fries and Belgian beer w/old world tavern interior & inn-style seating*

($$)

Corner Bistro (famous burger & beer special in classic Village pub, w4th/Jane)
[331 W 4th St] *famous NY Bistro burger that was tops on NY lists for decades, try the special of Bistro burger, fries and McSorley's beer, wooden booths in a well-maintained pub with a simple menu & good prices, cash only!*

John's of Bleecker St. (old time brick-oven pizzeria, Bleecker/Jones)
[278 Bleecker St] *classic NY brick oven pizza place since 1929 with highly-rated pizza, in a place with heavily scratched-up wooden booths & checkered floors, popular (serves only pies, not slices)*

La Bonbonniere Diner (old school NY diner, breakfast spot, 8th/w12th)
[28 8th Ave] *true NYC neighborhood diner that's as 60's & 70's old school as it gets, breakfast & lunch spot, blueberry pancakes, French toast, not as gourmet as other places in area but solid and roomy, also requires patience, cash only!*

Cotenna (cozy Italian restaurant, Bedford/Downing)
[21 Bedford St] *cozy small Italian restaurant w/intimate atmosphere, serves authentic Italian small specialty plates w/gnocchi, pastas, hanging smoked meats, date-perfect and reasonably priced with close quarter table dining & bar, well regarded*

Murray's Cheese Shop (famous cheese shop, sandwiches, Bleecker/Cornelia)
[254 Bleecker St] *famous cheesemonger in NY, bright well-ordered grocery store that's a mecca for all things cheese, has bread, olives, serves gourmet grilled cheese melts*

The Grey Dog (cafe/restaurant, American comfort food, w16th/8th)
[242 W 16th St] *the original Grey Dog, cozy rustic place with American comfort food, better for breakfast or lunch w/seating, Wifi, popular*

The Spaniard (stylish bar & gastropub, w4th/Barrow)
[190 W 4th St] *an elevated gastropub concept profiled by Architectural Digest, richly designed green leather booths w/reserved seating alongside an open bar, with exceptional food, large whiskey selection, chef has popular Smashburger, crowded on weekends*

($$$-$$$$)

Buvette Gastrotheque (fancy French bistro, popular brunch, Grove/Bleecker)
[42 Grove St] *upscale, fancy french gastrothèque-style bistro that's more like a fantasy version of French bistro - fine comfort foods, gourmet breakfast, brunch and dinner, attention to detail, wine selections w/bar area, walk-in only, pricey*

Boucherie West Village (popular French brasserie in West Village, Grove/Bleecker)
[99 7th Ave South] *bustling 320-seat French bistro & brasserie in a former repertory theater with a vine-terrace exterior and large space that is like stepping into old-time Paris, serving French classics like steak & frites, beef bourguignon, escargot, steak tartare, fun outdoor space & booths with lots of ambience*

Minetta Tavern (fancy tavern w/Black Label burger, MacDougal/MinettaLane)
[113 MacDougal St] *fancy old tavern known for its Black Label burger w/prime cuts of dry-aged beef, usually on top of multiple best NY burger lists, reservations or eat at the bar, pricey (Black Label burger @$40)*

Olio e Piú (old world Italian trattoria w/outdoor garden dining, Greenwich/6th)
[3 Greenwich Ave] *authentic Neapolitan Italian trattoria with Italian festive greenery, bistro tables, open terrace views of the Village w/Italian dishes, Neapolitan style thin crust pizza, pasta & wood-fire oven*

DRINKS & BARS

($$)

Blind Tiger Ale House (craft beer, Bleecker/Jones)
[281 Bleecker St] *craft beer bar located on one of best food streets in West Village, good selection of beer and excellent food in warm rustic-wooded interior, ideal place for lunch during quieter daytime hrs, gets crowded at night, popular & well regarded*

Arts and Crafts Beer Parlor (relaxed craft beer & gallery bar, w8th/MacDougal)
[26 W. 8th St] *craft beer & rotating art gallery in cozy wood lounge bar below street level w/art nouveau fireplace, laid back atmosphere & cheap happy hours, serves mostly drinks*

Vol de Nuit (small Belgian beer hall w/backyard patio garden, w4th/6th)
[148 W 4th St] *small dimly-lit beer hall focused on Belgian beers with European vibe, much like stepping into a side street bar in Brussels, serves Belgian fries w/small beer garden in back*

White Horse Tavern (old time tavern & dive bar, Hudson/w11th)
[567 Hudson St] *authentic NYC tavern & designated landmark that survives on its looks, cool name and great locale in a festive area of Village, once a watering hole for famous writers of NY's past, seating outside in nice weather, better for drinks, cash only!*

The Spaniard (stylish bar & gastropub, w4th/Barrow)
[190 W 4th St] *an elevated gastropub concept profiled by Architectural Digest, richly designed green leather booths w/reserved seating alongside an open bar with exceptional food, large whiskey selection, chef has popular Smashburger, crowded on weekends*

The Otherroom (dark and cozy wine & beer bar, Perry/Washington St)
[143 Perry St] *dimly-lit speakeasy with a chill vibe and lounge area, good for dates and after-dinner drinks by candlelight in an intimate space*

The Mermaid Oyster Bar (casual seafood oyster bar, MacDougal/Bleecker)
[89 MacDougal St] *casual, classy seafood restaurant focused on sustainably sourced seafood in nautically-decorated restaurant space, happy hours specials with mixed drinks & seafood appetizers*

SHOPPING

Three Lives & Company (independent bookstore, 10th/WaverlyPl)
[154 W 10th St] *quaint old neighborhood bookshop with new and used books in a picturesque store that's cozy to be in, nicely curated & well regarded*

Murray's Cheese Shop (famous cheese shop, sandwiches, Bleecker/Cornelia)
[254 Bleecker St] *famous cheesemonger in NY, bright well-ordered grocery store that's a mecca for all things cheese, has bread, olives, serves gourmet grilled cheese melts*

Goorin Bros. Hat Shop (hat shop, Bleecker/Christopher)
[337 Bleecker St] *family-owned hat store since 1895 for those seeking the perfect hat, selling contemporary & fitted hats*

Housing Works Thrift Shop West Village (thrift store, 10th/Hudson St)
[245 W 10th St] *good chain of NY thrift stores that are well ordered and pleasant to shop at, tend to sell affordable high end used clothes and stuff that reflects the neighborhood, has charitable mission behind it*

Small shops around neighborhood (Bleecker St, Hudson St, 8th Ave)
[West Village] *boutiques, specialty stores and whatnots scattered around the zig-zag old streets of the West Village, residential housing and shops are mixed together in some parts of the neighborhood that are off the main streets*

FUN STUFF

Film Forum (indie, classic & arthouse movie theater, W.Houston/Varick)
[209 W Houston St] *the main independent arthouse theater of NYC built in 1970, classic movies, art house, documentaries, has 3 small theaters plus a newer fourth theater that has a bigger 99-seat screening room added on after renovations, cinephiles come here more for the programming, popcorn is highly praised too*

Village Vanguard (famous NY jazz club, 7AveS/11th)
[178 7th Ave S] *legendary NYC jazz institution that was the top destination for jazz luminaries, still a place to come for jazz musicians that want to play in its famous basement surrounded by photos of all the greats, also known for its acoustics, buy tickets & cover per person w/one drink minimum, reservations are the better way to go*

Blue Note Jazz Club (iconic intimate jazz club in West Village, w3rd/6th)
[131 W 3rd St] *iconic jazz club attracting headline jazz acts to this intimate blue-lit space since its creation in 1981, seating is first-come first-serve with dining & bar service in a very tight-tabled venue (but close to stage), also has gift shop, buy tickets online*

Smalls (small & atmospheric Village jazz club, w10st/7thS)
[183 W 10th St] *small, intimate-spaced jazz club that's long been the place to go for jazz lovers, w/cover charge & drink minimum, highly regarded*

IFC Center movie theater(indie, classic and arthouse movie theater, 6th/w3rd)
[323 6th Ave] *centrally located indie movie theater in the Village that has 5 theaters with comfortable seats, plays classic movies and arthouse films, Netflix movies, documentaries, also hosts events & retrospectives*

MANHATTAN VIEWS

Hudson River Park (waterfront park by Hudson River, WestSt/10th)
[353 West St] *splendid river park on the Hudson River with biking and walking lanes, parks with waterfront views & many places to relax and picnic along the river taking in pictureque views of the city skyline or catching a sunset*

ATTRACTIONS

Washington Square Park (famous NY city park, people watching, w4th/5th)
[W 4th St] *famous city park in the heart of the Village featuring a grand plaza with the towering Washington Sq Arch at its entrance with a circular water fountain at its center - place to go for people-watching, to have lunch outside, enjoy street performers, play chess, catch events, picnic, meet up or just hang out*

Jazz Music Clubs
[West Village] *the West Village/Greenwich Village, along with Harlem, is known for being place in New York that is a destination for jazz lovers - jazz clubs like Village Vanguard, Blue Note & Smalls that make their home here to showcase the famous and up-and-coming on the jazz scene*

Foodie Destination
[West Village] *Bleecker Street, Hudson St, MacDougal St, Carmine St, W 10th St. The Village is known for having a consistent selection of good quality and gourmet restaurants, shops and eateries all around the neighborhood*

Hudson River Park (waterfront park by Hudson River, WestSt/10th)
[West St] *splendid river park on the Hudson River with biking and walking lanes, parks with waterfront views & many places to relax and picnic along the river taking in pictureque views of the city skyline or catching a sunset*

LGBTQ Community & Culture
[West Village/Greenwich Village] *along with San Francisco, the West Village and Greenwich Village have been historically rock solid centers for gay culture in the country and a welcoming destination spot for the LGBTQ community. It also played a historically significant role in the struggle for gay rights beginning with Stonewall Inn riots in 1969. The community's enthusiasm and continuous support for food, culture and the arts is evident by the high quality of restaurants, bars, coffee shops, jazz clubs, bookstores, shops and creativity in the area*

TRIBECA

quick directions
Take 1, 2, 3 downtown to Chambers St stop [Chambers/W.Broadway]

COFFEE

Kaffe Landskap NYC (South) (coffee shop, Greenwich/Murray)
[275 Greenwich St] *Scandinavian cafe with its own aesthetic, serves coffee, food & pastries w/wood bench seating, long tables, sheep decor, candles, dimly lit and spacious, Wifi*

Kaffe Landskap NYC (North) (coffee shop, Greenwich/Beach)
[401 Greenwich St] *Scandinavian cafe that's like contemporary artist's retreat with a long hall of wood benches, high ceilings & sheep decor, candles and ambience in a dimly lit, earthy rustic space, Wifi*

Interlude Coffee & Tea (coffee shop, Hudson/Hubert)
[145 Hudson St] *coffee shop with minimalist, sleek white interior - serves coffee, matcha lattes, tea, pastries in a light-filled open space w/seating & tables, a local favorite, Wifi*

La Colombe Coffee Roasters (coffee shop, Church/Lispenard)
[319 Church St] *upscale stylish coffee chain, serves coffee & pastries in urban brick wood interior with wide windows, seating & tables (no Wifi, no bathroom)*

TRIBECA

Laughing Man Coffee Company (coffee & tea shop, Duane/Greenwich)
[184 Duane St] *used to be a tiny grab & go in industrial loft neighborhood but now expanded into a bigger, roomy space in a distinctive Tribeca spot with a charitable mission behind it, popular flat white espressos, matcha lattes, also outdoor bench area plaza to relax in (no Wifi)*

Gotan Tribeca (cafe w/large & roomy space, Franklin/Varick)
[130 Franklin St] *cafe in a handsome, industrial loft brick space, serves coffee, gourmet sandwiches, salads, pastries, avocado toast, pastry, very roomy with lots of seating - tables, benches, booths, long tables, all have outlets, can do work or hang out, rare kind of comfortable lounge space in the city with amenities (no Wifi)*

TEA

Takahachi Bakery (Japanese bakery & cafe in Tribeca, Murray/Church)
[25 Murray S] *good-sized Japanese bakery and cafe w/Japanese hot food, bento boxes, matcha crepes, matcha lattes, desserts, baked on premises with cafe seating in back*

Interlude Coffee & Tea (coffee shop, Hudson/Hubert)
[145 Hudson St] *coffee shop with minimalist, sleek white interior - serves coffee, matcha lattes, tea, pastries in a light-filled open space w/seating & tables, a local favorite, Wifi*

Laughing Man Coffee Company (coffee & tea shop, Duane/Greenwich)
[184 Duane St] *used to be a tiny grab & go in industrial loft neighborhood but now expanded into a bigger, roomy space in a distinctive Tribeca spot with a charitable mission behind it, popular flat white espressos, matcha lattes, also outdoor bench area plaza to relax in (no Wifi)*

EATS

($)

Los Tacos No. 1 (authentic Mexican taco chain in NYC, Church/Warren)
[136 Church St] *Tribeca outpost of the highly rated authentic Mexican taco shop, often topping best of NYC lists, in a similar shop space to original Times Sq location i.e. the standing tables and decor, fun NYC experience, inexpensive*

Nish Nush (Mediterranean vegetarian food, falafel, Reade/Church)
[88 Reade St] *Mediterranean vegetarian eatery known for falafel platters, gourmet hummus in a roomy & inviting industrial wood space, open to street dining w/plenty of seating*

Takahachi Bakery (Japanese bakery & cafe in Tribeca, Murray/Church)
[25 Murray S] *good-sized Japanese bakery and cafe w/Japanese hot food, bento boxes, matcha crepes, matcha lattes, desserts, baked on premises with cafe seating in back*

($$)

Maman Tribeca (French American cafe & restaurant, W.Broadway/Franklin)
[211 W Broadway] *stylish French American cafe with elegant gourmet aesthetic, serving coffee, breakfast, brunch, bakery, food & setting in big Tribeca-sized space, Wifi*

Gotan Tribeca (cafe w/large & roomy space, Franklin/Varick)
[130 Franklin St] *cafe in a handsome, industrial loft brick space, serves coffee, gourmet sandwiches, salads, pastries, avocado toast, pastry, very roomy with lots of seating - tables, benches, booths, long tables, all have outlets, can do work or hang out, rare kind of comfortable lounge space in the city with amenities (no Wifi)*

Takahachi Tribeca (affordable Japanese sushi, Duane/W.Broadway)
[145 Duane St] *Japanese sushi place that's a neighborhood favorite, more affordable, down-to-earth w/good quality chef sashimi, well regarded*

($$$)

Smith & Mills (small plates restaurant & bar, N.Moore/Greenwich)
[71 N Moore St] *cozy small plates restaurant in a tiny crowded hole-in-the-wall place, looks like it's straight out of Travel+Leisure, gourmet food & Euro style, no reservations*

Tiny's & The Bar Upstairs (cozy restr, brkfst/brunch/bar, W.Broadway/Duane)
[135 W Broadway] *cozy restaurant, breakfast, brunch & bar in an old carriage house that dates back to the1800s, has time portal NY ambience with good food, date-friendly*

DRINKS & BARS

($)

Nancy Whiskey Pub (dive bar w/shuffleboard, Lispenard/W.Broadway)
[1 Lispenard St] *one of the diviest of old school dive bars with a shuffleboard table, cheap drinks, dilapidated upstairs wood bench seating, more fun if thirsty*

TRIBECA

($$)

Puffy's Tavern (pub w/Alidoro Italian sandwiches at lunch, Hudson/Harrison)
[81 Hudson St] *mellow neighborhood tavern, light-filled pub w/stylish tiled floor & darts, serves lunch special with Alidoro Italian sandwiches and Belgian beer on tap*

Anotheroom (dimly-lit craft beer bar, W.Broadway/Beach)
[249 W Broadway] *intimate, dimly-lit craft beer bar & lounge, low key place that's good for drinks with friends, a date or just chill in the dark, large craft beer selection, happy hours*

Smith & Mills (small plates restaurant & bar, N.Moore/Greenwich)
[71 N Moore St] *cozy small plates restaurant in a tiny crowded hole-in-the-wall place, looks like it's straight out of Travel+Leisure, gourmet food & Euro style, no reservations*

($$$)

Tiny's & The Bar Upstairs (cozy restr, brkfst/brunch/bar, W.Broadway/Duane)
[135 W Broadway] *cozy restaurant, breakfast, brunch & bar in an old carriage house that dates back to the1800s, has time portal NY ambience with good food, date-friendly*

SHOPPING

The Mysterious Bookshop (crime & mystery bookstore, WarrenSt/W.Broadway)
[58 Warren St] *bookshop dedicated to just crime & mystery books - used, new and rare books in a stacked-shelved old bookstore space, filled floor-to-ceiling with mystery books of all kinds - international crime novels, classic mysteries, murder mysteries, Agatha Christie novels, thrillers & capers, plus a dedicated Sherlock Holmes section*

Philip Williams Posters (poster shop, Chambers/W.Broadway)
[122 Chambers St] *old time poster shop that has vintage prints & posters in hall-spaced store that stretches from street to street covered floor to ceiling in posters, magazine covers, from expensive to cheap posters with all varieties*

Chambers Street Wines (wine shop, Chambers/W.Broadway)
[148 Chambers St] *neighborhood wine store in center of Tribeca with helpful staff and full selection of wines, well regarded*

Tribeca Greenmarket (small greenmarket on Wed & Sat, Greenwich/Chambers)
[Washington Market Park] *small greenmarket for local farms and produce, open Saturdays 8-2pm year round*

OUTDOOR PUBLIC SPACES

Many places to sit outside to have a coffee or a drink on cast-iron building dock fronts or benches, in the more industrial loft parts

Bogardus Plaza (outdoor city plaza w/seats, Hudson/Chambers)
[1 Hudson St] *outdoor plaza and pocket park w/patio table seating around garden & best starting point to explore the area - right in heart of Tribeca at Chambers St stop on 1 train*

Pier 25 - Hudson River Park (West Side Highway/N.Moore St)
[West Side Highway @ N Moore St] *Pier 25 and area around Hudson River waterfront park - has mini golf, skate park, beach volleyball courts, playgrounds for kids, biking and sweeping Hudson River & Manhattan views, especially at sunset*

FUN STUFF

Tribeca Film Festival 2024 (scheduled for June 5-16, 2024)
[tribecafilm.com] *Tribeca Film Festival takes place in multiple local movie theaters in the area from scheduled times listed on its website, scheduled for June 2024*

Roxy Cinema Tribeca (movie theater in Roxy Hotel, 6th/Church)
[2 6th Ave] *Art deco styled movie theater in basement of the Roxy Hotel that's modeled after the 1920's Roxy movie house - has one theater, serves gourmet concessions & cocktails, can use hotel lobby for drinks or to lounge, check schedule at roxycinemanewyork.com*

MANHATTAN VIEWS

Pier 25 - Hudson River Park (West Side Highway/N.Moore St)
[West Side Highway @ N Moore St] *Pier 25 and area around Hudson River waterfront park - has mini golf, skate park, beach volleyball courts, playgrounds for kids, biking and sweeping Hudson River & Manhattan views, especially at sunset*

TRIBECA

Fancy restaurants, wine bars, walk the neighborhood
[Tribeca] *Many places to sit outside cast-iron framed buildings, either on benches or stepped-out dock fronts of buildings in the industrial loft areas to have a coffee or drink. Shops, cafes, restaurants, wine bars and bars are interspersed throughout the area. Bogardus Plaza is one of the best starting points to explore Tribeca (located at the Chambers St stop on 1 train)*

Tribeca Film Festival 2024 (scheduled for June 5-16, 2024)
[tribecafilm.com] *Tribeca Film Festival takes place in multiple local movie theaters in the area from scheduled times listed on its website, scheduled for June 2024*

WALL STREET
Financial District

quick directions
Take 4, 5 downtown to Wall St stop [WallSt/Broadway]

COFFEE

Birch Coffee (coffee shop in Frank Gehry Building, Spruce/Nassau)
[8 Spruce St, entrance on Beekman] *roomy cafe on street floor of Frank Gehry building in FiDi, artfully designed, serves coffee, pastry in decent space w/wrap around window & center table seating (no Wifi)*

Black Fox Coffee Co. (big & roomy coffee shop, Pine/Pearl)
[70 Pine St] *big and roomy Australian cafe, serves pastries and food, solid place with plenty of seating (no Wifi)*

For Five Coffee Roasters (coffee shop in Brookfield Place, Liberty/S.EndAve)
[225 Liberty St] *modern & sleek coffee bar in large space at Brookfield Place, serves coffee, food, pastries, matcha lattes w/seating, can get long lines, Wifi (bathrooms in mall)*

La Colombe Coffee Roasters (stylish coffee shop, Wall/Pearl)
[67 Wall St] *upscale stylish coffee chain outpost in narrow space, serves coffee, pastries w/limited seating, grab & go (no Wifi, no bathroom)*

Blue Bottle Coffee (coffee shop near Sept 11th museum, Greenwich/Liberty)
[150 Greenwich St] *SF coffee roaster chain with cafe near the Sept 11th museum, pour-over coffee, in building corner space w/limited seating (no Wifi)*

Voyager Espresso (cafe in subway station lobby at John St, William/John)
[110 William St, lower level] *Aussie cafe in subway area with futuristic coffee bar that looks like it could be on a space station, serves espressos, well-made food, avocado toast, chia pudding w/bar stool seating, Wifi (no bathroom)*

TEA

Dragon Tea (Taiwanese bubble tea/milk tea cafe in FiDi, Greenwich/Carlisle)
[106 Greenwich St] *small, well-maintained Taiwanese bubble and milk tea shop in Financial District w/bubble teas, milk teas, fruit teas, smoothies & drinks*

EATS

($$)

Adrienne's Pizzabar (square pizza restaurant on festive Stone St, Stone/MillLane)
[54 Stone St] *square slice pizza restaurant that's a staple of Stone St, an old cobblestone street that gets festive, plentiful indoor & outdoor seating, popular (no slices, full pizza)*

Hudson Eats at Brookfield Place (food court w/waterfront views in Brookfield Place, Liberty/Southend)
[225 Liberty St] *fancy food court in Brookfield Place w/ocean views & outdoor patio space - Mighty Quinns BBQ, Dos Toros Taqueria, Dig market bowls, Starbucks & Blue Ribbon Sushi*

Le District (French food hall & marketplace in Brookfield Place, Liberty/Southend)
[225 Liberty St] *food hall inside Brookfield Place atrium by waterfront that's like a French version of Eataly with its own French cafe district, Market dining district and Garden district w/seating inside, also in the main glass atrium and outside by waterfront*

Eataly NYC Downtown (Italian gourmet food hall, Liberty/Church)
[101 Liberty St Fl 3] *downtown FiDi city glamour version of the Italian gourmet food hall - a big complex of markets, breads, cheese, seafoods, meats, pizza, pasta, groceries, restaurants w/seating & dynamic city views, popular eating destination*

La Parisienne Cafe (small French bistro cafe, MaidenLn/LibertyPl)
[9 Maiden Lane] *small and quaint French bistro cafe that's hard working and well liked, serving gourmet bistro food in a charming, no-frills white & teal decor w/seating*

Hole in the Wall (Australian cafe, breakfast/brunch, Cliff/Fulton)
[15 Cliff St] *popular Australian breakfast and brunch spot, well made gourmet food, open and spacious w/seating & outside patio*

Pisillo Italian Panini (authentic Italian sandwiches, Nassau/Ann)
[97 Nassau St] *popular deli in FiDi district with Italian panini sandwiches that gets a lunch crowd w/limited seating, well regarded in area, grab & go, cash only!*

The Malt House (American fare & craft beer in stylish tavern, MaidenLn/Broadway)
[9 Maiden Lane] *Tavern burgers, comfort food and American fare in a stylish exposed beams and brick tavern space with a modern bar area that has extensive whiskey & craft beer selection, ambient lighting, seating, long tables with a relaxed crowd that comes for the chill atmosphere*

Shake Shack - Fulton Transit Center- Manhattan (burger place, Broadway/Fulton)
[200 Broadway] *popular NYC burger chain, often on best burger list, located on Level 2 of rotunda in Fulton Center w/tables & views in spacious lounge seating*

Luke's Lobster FiDi (Maine lobster rolls, S.Williams/Broad)
[26 S William St] *cozy, rustic FiDi outpost of Luke's Lobster in a homey, nautical sea shack interior, popular lobster rolls and seafood w/seating*

Dig (farm fresh marketbowl, Pine/Pearl)
[80 Pine St] *fast casual food chain w/farm fresh marketbowl in rustic interior space, reliable place w/plenty of seating*

DRINKS & BARS

($$)

Ulysses Folk House (well known city tavern w/pub style food, Stone/William)
[58 Stone St] *good-sized dark and chunky wooden Irish tavern on Stone Street, serving ale & lager pints w/hearty pub fare, fresh oysters in a festive setting, live bands & street seating outside*

Heineken Riverdeck - Pier 17 (drinks w/views by Pier 17, SouthSt/Beekman)
[89 South St] *lounge bar with outdoor seating on Pier 17 with epic views of the Brooklyn Bridge, popular after-work place, opens in summer*

Mad Dog & Beans Mexican Cantina (festive after-work spot for Mexican food, homemade chips & guacamole, Pearl/Stone)
[83 Pearl St] *popular and festive Mexican restaurant/bar by Stone St with festive reclaimed wood decor, serving solid Mexican staples, margaritas, homemade chips & guacamole*

Hudson Eats & Le District in Brookfield Place (Liberty/Southend)
[225 Liberty St] *drinks & bars in high end shopping center with glass atrium and scenic views of the waterfront, especially within Hudson Eats & Le District eating areas where you can have drinks on the patio seating outside with harbor views*

The Malt House (American fare & craft beer in stylish tavern, MaidenLn/Broadway)
[9 Maiden Lane] *Tavern burgers, comfort food and American fare in a stylish exposed beams and brick tavern space with a modern bar area that has extensive whiskey & craft beer selection, ambient lighting, seating, long tables with a relaxed crowd that comes for the chill atmosphere*

($$$)
Dead Rabbit (fancy well-regarded multi-level Irish pub, Water/Broad)
[30 Water St] *cocktails and beer bar, woody industrial age tavern complex serves Irish food in mercantile NYC pub atmosphere, popular in Financial District*

SHOPPING

Westfield World Trade Center - The Oculus (shopping center, Greenwich/Fulton)
[185 Greenwich St] *modern space age mall at World Trade Center with the Oculus plaza at its center with big designer stores, eateries, Shake Shack & Apple store*

Brookfield Place (shopping center by water w/glass atrium, Vesey/West)
[230 Vesey St] *high end shopping center with giant glass atrium and scenic views of the waterfront, many stores with fancy luxury brands, eating areas like Le District & Hudson Eats that open up to waterfront patios and event areas*

FUN STUFF

Alamo Drafthouse Cinema (dine in/comfort movie theater, craft beer, Liberty/William)
[28 Liberty St] *fun movie theater experience located in basement levels of mall complex, bar & table seating in ticket lounge area w/selection of craft beers, 8 small intimate theater screens decked with reclining lounge chairs, food & drink service can be called by button or by written notes from chairs flagging attentive staff who help keep things pleasant and orderly while watching, shows classics, cult favorites & new movies*

Regal Cinemas Battery Park (movie theater, near Brookfield Pl, N.End/Vesey)
[102 North End Ave] *spacious, modern movie theater complex with comfy recliner seats, next to a Shake Shack and the Conrad Hotel, rarely crowded*

Bowling Green Greenmarket (small greenmarket, Bowling Grn/Broadway)
[1 Bowling Green] *solid little farmer's greenmarket at Bowling Green Plaza, from Apr to Dec - open Tue & Thu, 8am-2pm*

Midtown Comics Downtown (comic books, graphic novels, toys, Fulton/Gold)
[64 Fulton St, 2nd Fl] *downtown branch of Midtown Comics, the big comics store of Manhattan, upstairs space on Fulton St w/comics, graphic novels & collectibles*

Stone Street (old cobblestone street w/festive outdoor dining & drinking, Stone/William)
[Stone St] *a festive block on an old, narrow cobblestone street in FiDi w/outdoor picnic tables filled by people from its bars & restaurants, like a slice of outdoor Europe in Manhattan*

INDOOR PUBLIC SPACES

60 Wall Street Atrium (indoor public space, WallSt/HanoverSt)
[60 Wall St] *urban indoor public space, large area with patio seating, benches and tables w/coffee & subway nearby, Wifi*

OUTDOOR PUBLIC SPACES
& MANHATTAN VIEWS

Battery Park (scenic views in park near the ferries, Battery Place/StateSt)
[Battery Pl @ State St] *park in Financial District with scenic views of the Statue of Liberty and Ellis Island, walk around or relax on benches, free park Wifi*

Battery Park City Esplanade (scenic views of waterfront, Chambers to BatteryPl)
[Battery Park City, Chambers St to Battery Park] *scenic views of the Hudson River, Statue of Liberty and Ellis Island from walkway & esplanade - patio tables, chairs, benches, great for walking, running, especially at sunset, free park Wifi*

East River Waterfront Esplanade (scenic views, South St/Pier 11 to Pier 17)
[South St, from Pier 11 to Pier 17] *river walkway by East River from South Street Seaport to Pier 11, perfect for lunch or walks with waterfront views of Brooklyn Bridge*

One World Observatory (observatory w/NYC views, One World Trade Center)
[One World Trade Ctr, 117 West St] *observatory on 100th floor of One World Trade Center with sweeping panoramic sky views of NYC, @$44-$64 tickets*

Elevated Acre (urban open space plaza w/scenic views, WaterSt/SouthSt)
[55 Water St] *open space elevated park with large grass lawn to picnic or lie down in, patio tables and park seating all around the lawn to relax, have lunch and get away from the very compact FiDi with scenic waterfront views, free park Wifi*

The Rooftop @ Pier 17 (music venue w/views South St Seaport, SouthSt/Beekman)
[89 South St] *rooftop venue part of South St Seaport district on Pier 17, used mostly as a music venue that showcases epic views of Brooklyn Bridge & Manhattan skyline during performances, has skating rink in winter, can visit the rooftop just for its scenic views*

ATTRACTIONS

Wall Street (NY Stock Exchange, Charging Bull, Financial District, Wall/Broadway)
[Wall St] *visit well-known "Charging Bull" sculpture at Bowling Green/Broadway, walk around Financial District and NY Stock Exchange at Wall St & Broad St*

South Street Seaport District (mercantile walking district, SouthSt/Pier17)
[89 South St] *tourist destination & major attraction in FiDi with views from Pier 17, the historic old New York Mercantile Building Walking district with the iron-hulled Wavertree sailing ship in its harbor - a vessel built in 1885 that used to travel the world transporting goods*

9/11 Memorial Museum (museum about Sept 11th, Greenwich/Liberty)
[180 Greenwich St] *museum that commemorates Sept 11th at its memorial site, marked by two waterfalls at the base foundations of what used to be the Twin Towers of the former World Trade Center*

Ellis Island (history of immigration in US, at Whitehall Terminal, take ferry to island)
[4 South St, South Ferry at Battery Plaza] *major tourist attraction that's a former NYC immigration inspection station converted into a historical museum, dedicated to documenting the immigrant experience of those who came to America for a better life*

Statue of Liberty (top tourist attraction & world famous symbol of freedom with monument of Lady Liberty, take ferry to Liberty Island to visit)
[4 South St, South Ferry] *The Statue of Liberty or Lady Liberty, a gift from France in 1886 to mark the centennial of the birth of the nation, viewed as an international symbol of democracy and freedom, a top tourist attraction in NYC*

LINKS

 Leave us an honest review!
(scan the QR Code for link to book page)

If you got this book on Amazon and have a few minutes,
it would be great in so many ways to hear what you have
to say in a honest review. (A few words work too!)

 Visit our links at:
https://linktr.ee/funfunnewyork
(or just scan the QR Code)

See all our links on Linktree as they become available for our
website, books, NYC shop (bags, mugs, stickers , art prints,
carry-around maps), upcoming monthly newsletters & more.

 Sign up for our Monthly Newsletter
https://linktr.ee/funfunnewyork
(or just scan the QR Code)

Visit our Linktree to sign up for our Monthly Newsletter to
hear everything going on with Fun Fun New York, what's
new in our shops, books, discount coupons, prizes & more

 Get your own Fun Fun Map of NYC
https://linktr.ee/funfunnewyork
(or just scan the QR Code)

Order the Fun Fun Map you see in the book as a folded color,
carry-around map (or) you can order it as an art print.
As maps become available, you can order them on our Linktree
(linktree/funfunnewyork) and website (funfunnewyork.com)

funfunnewyork.com

NOTES

NOTES

NOTES

Made in United States
Orlando, FL
18 December 2024

56008239R00065